Posthumous Cantos

Ezra Pound (1885–1972) is one of the most influential, and contro-
versial, poets of the twentieth century. His poetry remains vital,
challenging, contentious, unassimilable.

Massimo Bacigalupo is an experimental filmmaker, scholar, translator
and literary critic. Since 1990 he has been Professor of American
Literature at the University of Genoa.

D1448512

Ezra Pound

Posthumous Cantos

Edited by Massimo Bacigalupo

CARCANET

First published in Great Britain in 2015 by

Carcanet Press Limited
Alliance House
Cross Street
Manchester
M2 7AQ

www.carcanet.co.uk

We welcome your comments on our publications
Write to us at info@carcanet.co.uk

Poems © Omar Pound and Mary de Rachewiltz, 2002
Editorial matter © Massimo Bacigalupo, 2015

First published in a binlingual edition in 2002 by Arnoldo Mondadori
Editore S.p.A., Milan

A CIP catalogue record for this book is available from the British Library

ISBN 978 1 784101 20 6

The publisher acknowledges financial assistance from Arts Council England

Typeset by XL Publishing Services, Exmouth
Printed and bound in England by SRP Ltd, Exeter

Contents

IV Voices of War, 1940–45

V Italian Drafts, 1944–1945

VI Pisa, 1945

VII Prosaic Verses, 1945–1960

VIII Lines for Olga, 1962–1972

Introduction

Ezra Pound devoted much of his life to the writing of a long poem, *The Cantos*, which was to be a history both of the world and of himself, a new *Odyssey* telling the story of an exile's return to his home and promised land, and a new *Divine Comedy* depicting the arduous ascent from Hell to an erotic and visionary Paradise. However, while those great models were based on a linear narrative, Pound, a poet of the image and of sudden intuitions, tells his story circularly, by repetition and variation. The part contains the whole, and canto 1 already offers a blueprint for the entire poem, going from Odysseus's descent to Hades to a vision of Venus, she of 'dark eyelids', as well as 'mirthful'. She is Baudelaire's beautiful temptress, revisited by an American poet who arrived in Europe with an insatiable desire for knowledge and self-affirmation.

Consequently, over the fifty-year course of Pound's poem, states of mind alternate, and the only continuous and irreversible story that we can make out in its turbulent pages is the poet's own life, his travels and sudden departures, his pitfalls and misadventures, his aesthetic youth, his maturity increasingly occupied by economic projects, the day of reckoning of his incarceration, the relatively serene twilight of his final years.

Pound always wrote with incisiveness and passion, and the best parts of *The Cantos* are an eccentric but powerful chronicle of his times and of some of their most representative figures. The troubadour and friend of Yeats of the London salons; the Renaissance scholiast and guru of Shakespeare and Company, the Paris bookshop patronized by Joyce and Hemingway; the passionate tennis player and compiler of ABCs (*How to Read*, *Guide to Kulchur*, *ABC of Economics*), perfectly naturalized in Rapallo during the two decades of Fascism; the desperate and unregenerate prophet of the Pisan cage; and finally that painful persona – the poet in the insane asylum of Washington, DC, not far from the White House and its tenant, to whom he believed he had much to impart. These are images known to everyone, images that do not, and will not, cease to provoke fear and wonder, as well as delight, like the mirthful Venus of canto 1.

The Cantos began among false starts and revisions between 1915 and 1925, when they first appeared in a book-length sequence, *A Draft of XVI Cantos* – a title still suggesting tentativeness, though cantos 1–16 were to remain substantially unchanged in later editions. In 1917 Pound published in *Poetry*, the groundbreaking Chicago monthly of which he was European correspondent, 'Three Cantos', a rich and brilliant overture to his long poem, devoted in part to a debate with himself on 'what's left for me to do', in part to descriptions of cherished landscapes (chiefly Sirmione on Lake Garda) and to extracts from, and comments on, his omnivorous reading (Lorenzo Valla; Catullus; the Chinese poets, who were a recent enthusiasm). The last of 'Three Cantos' was for the greater part a version of Book XI of the *Odyssey*, the descent to Hades of Ulysses to consult Tiresias – a version, as the poet-scholar notes, based not on Homer's original but on a Latin crib published in 1538. Why so? Essentially because Pound always uses the material at hand, and perhaps Latin was easier for him to read – and misread – than Greek. Through the travesty of a double translation it might be possible to recover the foreignness and potency of the original. Yet Pound's main conceit here was the use in his version of the rhythms and alliterations of the Old English *Seafarer* and *Wanderer*, which he had admired at college. The result is a music touched by archaism, a neo-medievalism that blends with classicism and modernism in a characteristic Poundian pastiche: history is present in the layers of the text. As for subject-matter, Odysseus's encounter with the dead is a metaphor of Pound's own confrontation with friends lost in the First World War, which he experienced as a non-combatant in London, in a period of intense productivity, possibly enhanced by that great European tragedy. It also alludes to Dante's otherworldly travels and encounters, and suggests that *The Cantos* will be a summoning of ghosts, from whom much will be learned about our present and future.

Between 1917 and 1922, the 'Three Cantos' of 1917 were followed by nine further cantos, numbered progressively, but when in 1923 Pound gave quasi-final form to cantos 1–16 for book publication, he radically revised the overture, with the same decisiveness he had brought one year before to the manuscript of T. S. Eliot's *The Waste Land*. The descent to Hades of the third canto became, with appropriate cuts, canto 1, thus providing a grandiose though precarious introduction to all that follows. 'Canto I' and 'Canto II' of 1917 were also broken up, rearranged and augmented. The poem resulting from these radical changes was more experimental. Pound no longer detained his readers with doubts and perplexities about his intentions: he said what he had to say, and stopped. In this way, despite some uncertainties, the ship of *The Cantos* was launched, not to be overshadowed for esotericism and experimentalism by those two coeval cruisers – *Ulysses* and *The Waste Land*.

However, not all was gain in the transition from 'Three Cantos' to *XVI Cantos*. Pound was more confidential and sympathetic in the early version, with his student's literary passions, his portrait of the not very young artist (he was over thirty), his not invariably persuasive anecdotes (this was not to change in the final version), and his infectious lyric breakthroughs. But the 1917 'Three Cantos' remained forgotten in the back files of *Poetry* (and in the volumes *Lustra* and *Quia Pauper Amavi* of 1917–1919), to be reprinted only after Pound's death. Thus they can be justifiably included in a book titled *Posthumous Cantos*.

After this uncertain start, *The Cantos* proceeded without too many obstacles. Pound had found a canto-style and he went on to perfect it and modify it over the decades. But given the composite nature of his project, which is made up of autobiography, history and economics, evocations of moments of immersion in nature and physical and mental delight (the gods), translations of and annotations on Cavalcanti, Dante and the ancient Confucian annals – given all this, the text of *The Cantos* as it appeared in a series of installments (called 'decads' by Pound, though often containing not ten but eleven cantos, sometimes more) is the result of an extensive process of writing and rewriting. Pound wrote lines and passages in notebooks or on stray sheets, then typed and retyped his notes, and was often dissatisfied with first drafts. The 'canto', as the name suggests, had to be a kind of composition, or talk, moving on without breaks from opening to close. Pound drafted a canto and if he was not happy with the result he started again from the beginning. This explains in part the notorious obscurity of Pound, who as he wrote and rewrote the same passages forgot, or decided he could do without, this or that clarification. Let the readers worry. He had more important matters to attend to, nothing less than 'the tale of the tribe', as he called his poem. (In the meantime he had become enthusiastic about Leo Frobenius and African civilizations.) Surprisingly enough, Pound carefully preserved his notebooks and drafts, perhaps thinking that he could make use of them later. (He surely did not anticipate that university libraries in his native land would vie for their possession.) Thus the text of *The Cantos* as published is only the tip of an iceberg of mostly unpublished material: notebooks, typescripts, proofs. At times Pound really forgot memorable passages among his drafts, though generally he proved a good judge in choosing what to preserve and what to discard.

The present volume offers a selection from this abundant material, based on criteria of quality, accessibility, and documentary interest. Passages from the inter-war years are relatively few because the best writing appears to have made it into *The Cantos* as we have them. The early lines about Pound's meeting with Eliot in Verona (*By the arena, you, Thomas amics*) offer a sketch of an encounter that was to find its place, more allusively, in the *Pisan Cantos*, and give an idea of Pound's method. (It is striking how rough and journal-like these notes are, even mentioning 'Bitter Bonomelli', a popular drink in Italian cafés of the period.) Similarly, the three discarded openings of what was to become canto 2 (*And So-shu stirred in the sea*) show us the poet at work, sketching, abbreviating and even eliminating entire segments, some of them notable, as he seeks both themes and procedures. Of great interest are three such passages that appeared in various drafts of canto 49, the often-cited 'Seven Lakes Canto' on Chinese themes. This originally had an anecdotal prologue (two distinct and striking versions) and included a long and distasteful invective, wisely omitted by Pound. This is the period in which Pound wrote his celebrated 'Usura' canto, denouncing with Ruskinian fervour the destruction that bad economic practices brought to the pre-Raphaelite 'world of moving energies', and to great art and artists. He repeated the theme in canto 51 (for 'repetita juvant'), a canto for which we have many discarded passages, some of them linking Pound's usurious foes (John Law, founder of the bank of France) and his musical friends (Antonio Vivaldi) against a Venetian background. At the same time he was attempting to reconstruct in his poem the unspoiled pre-capitalist world in which nature and culture coalesce, and he found it in the ancient customs that he noted among his peasant neighbours in Rapallo (the town near Genoa where Pound spent much of his writing life). These he describes excitedly in drafts dealing with nature, folklore, and sexuality, preliminary to the well-known, and somewhat truculent, 'fertility cantos' (39 and 47).

With the war, the development of the poem entered upon a more turbulent and poetically productive phase. Pound did not grasp at first the enormity of events, or what his collaboration with the Italian state radio would cost him. In 1940 he had published *Cantos LII–LXXI* and he was already envisaging a final volume devoted to religion and philosophy. Many notes, here titled *Voices of War*, evoke nature rituals going back to Greek myth, but they are interspersed with reports of contemporary disasters, among them the testimony of a veteran of the war in Greece. One draft was of special interest to me, for it opens with an anecdote about my grandfather (and namesake), who operated a pharmacy in Rapallo. In August 1943 (as we learn from the draft) he lent Ezra the bound volume of the *Gazzetta di Genova* for 1815, which he happened to possess and was showing to his friends in the shop. Pound carried this precious find to his attic apartment on the Rapallo seafront, and began making notes of events surrounding Napoleon's Hundred Days – that is, his brief return to power after the Elba exile – implying a parallel with the arrest of Mussolini (July 1943) and possibly with his rescue by the Germans, that led to the creation of the puppet Republic of Salò (1943–45).

Again, Pound could not imagine the consequence of these events and how much he and his poem would be overwhelmed by them. The notion of a fearless last stand against all enemies, with anarchic and antibourgeois components, attracted Pound as much as Marinetti, his Futurist antagonist and associate, and both reaffirmed their allegiance to their contemporary Mussolini in his pathetic and bloody decline. Pound wrote articles for the newspapers of the Repubblica Sociale Italiana (as the Salò Republic was called), published economic and historical pamphlets in Rapallo and Venice, and even composed two cantos in Italian (cantos 72–73) to salute the 'boys' and 'girls' who 'wear black' (i.e., the Fascist black shirt). Part of canto 72 and all of canto 73 appeared in a fugitive periodical of the 'Republican Navy' (*Marina Repubblicana*), to be included only in 1985 in the full edition of *The Cantos* issued in Italy for the Pound centenary. (In 1986 they were added to the US edition.) From every point of view, cantos 72–73 are astonishing: an American writing in quasi-medieval Italian of El Alamein, Ezzelino da Romano (who figures in Dante), Marinetti, and that 'half-foetus who sold all of Italy and the Empire' (the proverbially diminutive King of Italy, who dismissed Mussolini). What chiefly strikes the reader is Pound's passion – and passion is what invigorates these texts.

Thus *The Cantos* could do anything – they could speak also in tragic times, of yesterday as well of today. Isolated as he was in the hills overlooking Rapallo, Pound planned further Italian poems, producing a quantity of tentative drafts. Here he wrote of visions he had encountered or imagined along the hillpaths, of Medieval and Renaissance figures, as well as of stray deranged women whose homes had been destroyed. They were Cunizza (another favourite Dante persona), the Moon, the Madonna of the Ligurian sea-shrines, and Isotta, beloved of Malatesta, whose 'Temple' in Rimini had been damaged by Allied attacks. (Rimini was on the 'Gothic Line', which in 1944–45 separated the Allies in the South of Italy from the Germans and their Fascist allies in the North.) Pound worked as indefatigably as always on these drafts, which also included a potted history of the Roman empire and meetings with further ghosts (among them Basinio, Malatesta's court poet, and Scotus Erigena, the Carolingian philosopher). When on May 3, 1945, two partisans arrested him in his hillside retreat, these pages were on his desk. He never returned to them, the captive Italian audience for *The Cantos* having dissolved in the interim; instead he returned to English and composed his most celebrated and controversial work, the eleven Pisan cantos (74–84). But Pound the professional poet never wasted anything: remembered passages from the Italian drafts recur in the Pisan sequence, recalling that visionary period of suspension before the catastrophe. Here I offer a selection of these rather rough Italian drafts, with an English translation which I hope will allow readers to appreciate their mixture of historic drama and otherworldliness. (Buddha, Confucius and the Madonna of the Assumption of the hilltop shrines all figure together in Pound's syncretic elysium.)

Unlike the Italian drafts of 1945, which came to fruition only as material for later use, the Pisan cantos reveal few second thoughts in the transition from notebook to typescript to print. In the relative quiet (the quiet after the storm) of the US Army disciplinary camp, Pound was able to write a prison journal in verse which was also a justification for his life and a realization of the project of *The Cantos*, which at this point (as mentioned above) was supposed to turn to philosophy and religion. The prisoner's stream of consciousness is interspersed with visionary episodes, true celebrations of the rituals of Venus, Diana-Luna, the Sun, Dionysus – the latter present through the god's and Pound's totem-animal, the lynx.

Pound wrote slowly but steadily through the summer, noting the changes of the season, from the oppressive July heat to the November hoarfrost. He deleted little of what he composed, the major exception being a long passage from the end of the last Pisan canto (84), and its 6-line prologue, a kind of formal testament, very explicit and emotional (*Yet from my tomb such flame of love arise*). He may have cancelled the latter because too personal and old-fashioned, or of ill omen ('my tomb'). For all he knew, he could have been hanged, or electrocuted, for his 'treason'. The deletion of the last pages results in a briefer and stronger conclusion to the Pisan sequence, so that the poet exits with new-found bravado – no tearful farewells. Pound never repented, except, at moments, for his personal failings.

During the years of his detention at St Elizabeths Hospital (1945–58), Pound composed two further volumes of cantos (or 'cantares', as he now called them). These are written in the Pisan style, but give little attention to their surroundings. Perhaps the confinement of the madhouse enters the poem in other ways, and at times one suspects that Pound's crumb of folly has grown to full-scale paranoia. (What better proof of a conspiracy did he need than his own incarceration?) At any rate, *The Cantos* continue to present his version of world history, and he no longer intends to close with canto 100, as Dante had done: while there is the poem to be written there is life and hope.

From this period we also have notebooks and drafts with passages that were not used in the published text. One such document is a long typewritten transcript of notebooks from the early Washington years, preliminary to cantos 85–95. These cantos appeared with the title *Rock-Drill* after Pound gave them final form in 1954, in the course of a few particularly fruitful and creative months. From this typescript nine extracts are offered here. In 1959 Pound himself made a similar yet briefer selection for a minuscule Italian pamphlet, *Versi prosaici* – hence the appropriate title of this section, *Prosaic Verses*.

One prominent future, not wholly new to be sure, is the ubiquity of quotations, as if the world of discourse were made up of the sayings of others, offered as authoritative. It is a paradox of Pound's self-centered world (*The Cantos* can be read as an autobiographical myth), that to create his lopsided spider's web he deploys fragments of 'reality', which mostly are nothing of the sort.

Pound had more trouble in concluding the next volume of cantos, *Thrones 96–109*. For example, canto 100, which one would expect to carry special significance, is chiefly composed of left-over notes from 1951–52, which makes for an anticlimax. But this may be one of the old poet's tricks. He had returned to Italy in 1958 and the euphoria attendant on freedom regained soon gave way to exhaustion and depression, so that he was unable to conclude to his satisfaction a final volume of cantos, 110–116. (It appeared in 1968, edited by his publisher from drafts written no later than 1960.) The volcano which had not stopped throwing out sublimities and fatuities over sixty years was finally spent, or quiescent. He had found a quiet haven in the care of his lifelong companion Olga Rudge, from whom he had been estranged from 1954 to 1962. Feeling guilty for this betrayal, and suffering from acute depression, he became convinced that Olga was making inordinate personal and economic sacrifices for his sake – while in fact she was happy to shoulder the burden of living with her great man, and to do all she could in order that the world grant him the homage his genius deserved. In this state of mind, Pound wrote for Olga a number of plangent fragments, like an old man's love notes, full of tenderness and admiration, recalling moments of their life together (even their first meeting at a masked ball in Paris), and crediting her with a clarity of perception that he might have lacked. Thus his praise also has ethical import, and is of a kind with the paradise of *The Cantos*, which, though marred by grievous errors, at least tries to avoid solipsism. And so Venus, as foreshadowed in canto 1, returns at the end, with her golden ornaments and her mirth, the vanquisher of monsters, 'bearing the golden bough of Argicida'.

Massimo Bacigalupo

Note on the English Edition

The present collection of unpublished and uncollected texts by Ezra Pound is based on the Italian edition, *Canti postumi*, published by Mondadori of Milan in 2002, with the addition of English translations (by me) of drafts originally written (and here presented) in Italian, and of the following passages (sources for which are indicated in the Notes): *Das endlich eine wirkliche Verständigung; Work is not a commodity. No one can eat it; Maderno, and there was calm in the stillness; a quando?; L'arif est gai, de bonne humeur, souriant; Out of Earth into tree; the madness & cancer are nothing; The gondolas dying in their sewers; and as to why this timing?* Pound's writings have been checked against the originals, so there are numerous variants, corrections, and additions to the Italian edition. The Pound papers are mostly housed in the Beinecke Rare Book and Manuscript Library at Yale University, which granted me a fellowship in 1988. Some of the results of that research were published in Italian journals, in the book *Je rassemble les membres d'Osiris* (Tristram, 1989), and in *Paideuma* 20.1–2 (1991) and 30.1–2 (2001). In 1988 my late friend Maria Costanza De Luca was planning a facsimile edition of the source of the Seven Lakes Canto (canto 49), so I looked up for her the drafts of that famous Chinese pastiche and found that it was originally prefaced by a striking prologue concerning Lord Byron and Henry James at Portovenere and the inscription on the so-called Grotta Byron in the village (see below, *'From this grotto'*). The inscription cited by James and Pound did not quite correspond to the present one – a discrepancy due (I found out) to the fact that the original tablet was replaced with a new one in the 1950s. In 2005 I visited the Grotta Byron with Seamus Heaney and photographed him standing under its portal and tablet.

This made him the fourth towering (and fun-loving) presence to have paused in front of this Grotto dedicated to Apollo but chiefly to Venus. This is the kind of adventure that Pound's writings move us to undertake – adventures mostly among texts, since Pound was a great and erratic transcriber of written records, but happily also among hill-towns and seascapes. None could be more delightful and inspiring than the Portovenere promontory, overlooking, as James wrote, 'the tideless sea' – just across the bay from Shelley's 'tragic villa' in Lerici. So, when in 2001 I collected some short pieces on writers and their ambience, I titled the book *Grotta Byron*. What better image of the 'apostolic succession' of which Pound is a major link: Shelley, Byron, James, Pound, Heaney... They were all travellers, readers, contempla-tives, lovers of the gifts of the world.

These presences have been important during the preparation of this collection, which begins with Pound telling us excitedly of Sirmione, on Catullus's Lake Garda, and inviting us to follow him in his discoveries. Later the atmosphere darkens considerably, and *The Cantos* and their drafts record some of the greatest tragedies of the century, and may be said to be complicit with their perpetrators. However, 'no one is guiltless', as another poet who knew and appre-ciated Pound, Eugenio Montale, wrote in his 'The Hitlerian Spring'. Pound never tires of seeking the golden thread in the pattern, and often, in *The Cantos* as in these fragments, we come 'out of heaviness where no mind moves at all', into 'light air, under saplings'. Perhaps it is one of the merits of this poetry that it doesn't understate the diffi-culties of the journey, doesn't allow us to 'get through hell in a hurry' (canto 46). Most important, since we are dealing with verse, Pound's words remain in our memory, as just representations of emotions, as inventions added to the trove of the language. In 1956 an Italian scholar and friend of Pound, Carlo Izzo, described him to Eliot as 'the greatest living creator of language', with which assessment, Izzo reported to Pound, the prudent Mr Eliot 'seemed to agree' (*Nuova Corrente* 148 (2011), p. 185).

In conclusion, I wish to thank Mary de Rachewiltz, who has been a supporter of this project from the beginning, and told me that she would like to see an English edition. After all, it is surprising, as well as indicative, that a book of uncollected and unpublished verse by so major a figure should be available to an Italian audience but not to readers in England and America, the countries with which Pound had very much a lover's quarrel. The quarrel is doubtless the explanation. I am grateful to Carcanet for undertaking this edition, which will go down as another adventure in the complicated publishing history of Ezra Pound (everything concerning him seems to be a little complicated). For making available to me heretofore unpublished material I am thankful to Walter Baumann, Ron Bush and Richard Sieburth. Michael Alexander and Martin Dodsworth were kind enough to read the texts and apparatus, and made helpful suggestions.

The Italian edition was dedicated to my parents Giuseppe and Frieda Bacigalupo, who in their roles as doctors and friends were always (I wrote) 'generous to EP – and to me'. ('Magnanimity / magnanimity / I know I ask a great deal', as Pound puts it here.) Early on I contracted a debt with Olga Rudge and Dorothy and Ezra Pound, who put up with my youthful impertinence. In 1962 Pound wrote self-effacingly in my copy of *XXX Cantos*, the beautiful and accurate Scheiwiller edition translated by his daughter, 'Hoping Massimo may find some good in it somewhere'. This volume should prove that Pound has not ceased to intrigue and delight over half a century.

M.B.

Chronology

1885

October 30: Ezra Pound born in Hailey, Idaho, to Homer Pound (1858–1942) and Isabel Weston (1860–1948).

1887

Family moves to New York and (June 1889) to Philadelphia.

1898

Summer trip to Europe with mother and great aunt Frank Weston: London, Brussels, Cologne, Bingen, Lucerne, Milan, Genoa, Pisa, Rome, Naples, Florence, Venice, Como, Paris.

1901–03

Admitted to University of Pennsylvania; takes courses in Liberal Arts. Meets William Carlos Williams and Hilda Doolittle.

1902

Second European summer tour with Aunt Frank and parents: Granada, Gibraltar, Tangiers, Venice, London.

1903

Transfers to Hamilton College, Clinton, NY. Studies Romance languages with William P. Shepard.

1905

May: 'Belangal Alba' published in *Hamilton Literary Magazine*. Graduates as Bachelor of Philosophy. Returns to University of

Pennsylvania; takes courses in Romance languages and literatures with Hugo Rennert.

1906

April–June: Travels to Europe on fellowship: Gibraltar, Madrid, Paris, London.

June 13: MA in Romanics, University of Pennsylvania.

September: Publishes first article.

1907–08

Instructor of Romance languages, Wabash College, Crawfordsville, Indiana.

1908

March 17: Sails from New York to Gibraltar.

April: Proceeds by ship from Gibraltar to Genoa. Travels in Northern Italy (Pavia, Verona). Settles in Venice.

July: *A Lume Spento* (poems) self-published in Venice.

August: Arrives in London, where he remains until 1920.

December: *A Quinzaine for this Yule: Being Selected from a Venetian Notebook* published by Elkin Mathews.

1909

Lectures at London Regent Street Polytechnic on 'Development of Literature in Southern Europe'. Meets W. B. Yeats through Olivia Shakespear.

September: Moves to 10 Church Walk, Kensington.

Personae. Exultations.

1910

Second series of lectures at Polytechnic, on 'Medieval Literature'.

March–May: In Paris, Venice and Sirmione on Lake Garda.

June: Travels to the US.

The Spirit of Romance (prose). *Provença.*

1911

February: Returns permanently to Europe, not to revisit the US until 1939.

March–May: In Paris with Walter Morse Rummel, Margaret

Cravens, and Yeats.

July: Sirmione, Verona, Mantua, Goito, Milan (Biblioteca Ambrosiana).

August: In Freiburg-im-Breisgau to discuss Arnaut Daniel with professor Emil Lévy. Visits Ford Madox Hueffer (Ford) in Giessen, Germany.

November: Begins collaboration (1911–36) with London journal *New Age*, edited by A. R. Orage; writes series of articles 'I Gather the Limbs of Osiris'.

Christmas at Salisbury with Maurice Hewlett.

Canzoni.

1912

May–July: Paris and walking tour in Southern France.

September–November: 'Patria Mia', a series of twelve articles, in *New Age*.

October: Begins collaboration (1912–62) with *Poetry* magazine, edited in Chicago by Harriet Monroe.

Ripostes. Sonnets and Ballate of Guido Cavalcanti.

1913

April–May: Paris, Sirmione. Meets Richard Aldington and H.D. in Venice.

Summer: Associates with Wyndham Lerwis and sculptor Henri Gaudier-Brzeska.

November: Filippo Tommaso Marinetti promotes Futurism in London. Pound may have met him at Yeats's on this or another occasion.

December: At Stone Cottage, Sussex, as secretary to Yeats. (Further periods at Stone Cottage in winter 1915 and 1916.)

December 15: On Yeats's recommendation, initiates correspondence (1913–37) with James Joyce.

1914

Edits the anthology *Des Imagistes*.

April 20: Marries Dorothy Shakespear (1886–1973). Moves to 5 Holland Place Chambers, Kensington.

June 20: *Blast: A Review of the Great English Vortex*, edited by Wyndham Lewis, published in London, includes poems and prose by Pound.

September: Meets T. S. Eliot.

1915

December 18: Writes to his father that he has drafted several cantos of a 'big long endless poem', and advises him to read Browning's *Sordello*.

Cathay.

1916

Gaudier-Brzeska: A Memoir. Lustra.

Cuala Press of Dublin issues *Certain Noble Plays of Japan, From the Manuscripts of Ernest Fenollosa, Chosen and Finished by Ezra Pound, With an Introduction by William Butler Yeats.*

1917

June–August: 'Three Cantos' appear in *Poetry*.

September: US edition of *Lustra*, including 'Three Cantos'.

'Noh' or Accomplishment: A Study of the Classical Stage of Japan by Ernest Fenollosa and Ezra Pound.

1918

Pavannes and Divisions (prose).

1919

April–September: With Dorothy in Toulouse, Provence and Paris. In August Eliot joins the Pounds in Excideuil.

Quia Pauper Amavi (includes 'Homage to Sextus Propertius' and 'Three Cantos').

The Fourth Canto privately issued by John Rodker in London.

1920

May–July: Paris and Venice, where he begins 'Indiscretions', a series of autobiographical sketches for *New Age*.

June 8: Meets James and Giorgio Joyce in Sirmione.

Begins collaboration (1920–29) with *The Dial*, published monthly in New York.

December: The Pounds move to Paris, 70bis rue Notre Dame des Champs.

Instigations (prose). *Hugh Selwyn Mauberley. Umbra: The Early Poems.*

1921
January–March: On French Riviera (Saint-Raphaël).
September: Contributes first of a series of 'Paris Letters' (1921–23) to *The Dial*.
Poems 1918–1921: Including Three Portraits and Four Cantos [IV–VII].

1922
January 3: During Paris visit, Eliot shows him typescript of *The Waste Land*; Pound makes suggestions for cuts and improvements.
March–June: With Dorothy in Siena, Perugia, Assisi, Ancona, Rimini, Venice and Rapallo, where they return at year's end.
Late May or early June: Meets T. S. Eliot and Bride Scratton 'by the arena' in Verona.
October 28: Mussolini's 'March on Rome' and subsequent seizure of power. 'Fascist Era' to date from this day.
Autumn: Meets violinist Olga Rudge (Youngstown, Ohio, 1895–Tirolo di Merano, 1996) in Natalie Clifford Barney's salon at 20 rue Jacob, Paris.

1923
January–February: In Rapallo with Ernest and Hadley Hemingway. Tours Tuscany with the Hemingways in the steps of Sigismondo Malatesta. Visits the Biblioteca Malatestiana of Cesena and is befriended by director, Manlio Torquato Dazzi.
March: In Rimini, at Palace Hotel, whose owner Averardo Marchetti becomes a friend.
Begins collaboration with T. S. Eliot's *Criterion*, which prints the four 'Malatesta Cantos' in the July issue.
Indiscretions issued as a book by William Bird at Three Mountains Press, Paris.
August: Walking tour in Dordogne with Olga Rudge.

1924
May: Perugia and Assisi.
October: In Rapallo. *Antheil and The Treatise of Harmony.*
December: Taormina.

1925

January: Meets Yeats in Syracuse, Sicily. *A Draft of XVI Cantos* published by Three Mountains Press, with illustrations by Henry Strater.

February: Writes from Palermo to his mother: 'I think Rapallo is about as good a port as one is likely to find'.

March: Takes attic apartment on the Rapallo seafront in Via Marsala, 12 (today no. 20, apt. 5).

June 6: Writes in Italian to critic Carlo Linati: '*XVI Cantos* is perhaps the first American book in which author, engraver and printer collaborated to create a whole. Since they could not construct another Parma Baptistery, since they don't have the money for a unity of the arts in an architectonic structure, they have chosen to reunite three arts in one small thing: drawings and capitals, as in the manuscripts of the Middle Ages'.

May 26: Deposits copy of *A Draft of XVI Cantos* in the Biblioteca Malatestiana, Cesena.

July 9: Daughter Maria born to Olga Rudge in Bressanone-Brixen.

December 19–23: T. S. Eliot visits the Pounds in Rapallo.

1926

May 6: Olga Rudge and composer Alfredo Casella perform music by Satie and Pound at Sala Sgambati, Rome.

June: Extracts from Pound's opera *Le Testament* premiered in Paris.

September 10: Omar Shakespear Pound, Dorothy's son, born in Paris.

December 22: *Personae: The Collected Poems* published in New York by Boni & Liveright.

1927

February: Olga Rudge and pianist Daniele Amfitheatrof play Mozart and Antheil in Rome, first at Sala Capizucchi, then in private concert for Mussolini.

April: Ernest Hemingway and Guy Hickok visit the Pounds in Rapallo. Hickok reports in *Brooklyn Daily Eagle*, 17 April 1927: 'Ezra Pound, American Author, Now in Genoa, Has Regular Bathtub and Charming Wife'.

Edits in Rapallo two issues of little magazine *The Exile* (spring and autumn). Receives *Dial* Award.

1928

February: W. B. Yeats arrives with family in Rapallo, and rents apartment until spring 1930. In the autumn Yeats works on *A Packet for Ezra Pound*, published by Cuala Press in June 1929, and reprinted in *A Vision*.

Autumn: Olga Rudge buys rooms in Venice (Calle Querini, 252 Dorsoduro). In following years Pound joins Olga and Mary in Venice for part of summer.

A Draft of Cantos 17–27. *The Exile*, issues 3–4. *Ta Hio: The Great Learning* (translation of classic Confucian text). *Selected Poems*, edited by T. S. Eliot.

1929

January: 'How To Read, or Why' (articles in *New York Herald Tribune*, collected as pamphlet in 1931).

June: Homer and Isabel Pound arrive in Rapallo and settle permanently.

Basil Bunting in Rapallo until 1933.

1930

April: Begins collaboration (1930–32) with *L'Indice* of Genoa, monthly literary tabloid edited by Gino Saviotti. Olga rents the top floor of a house in the village Sant'Ambrogio, on the hill between Rapallo and Zoagli.

May 25: Attends Frankfurt premiere of George Antheil's opera *Transatlantic*.

Summer: Visits Venice Biennale of Contemporary Art and praises Futurist pavilion ('Venezia bella', *Indice*, February 1931).

August: *A Draft of XXX Cantos* published in limited edition by Nancy Cunard at Hours Press, Paris.

1931

October 26–27: *The Testament of François Villon*, words and music by Ezra Pound, broadcast by BBC. Begins work on second radio opera, *Cavalcanti*.

1932

January: *Guido Cavalcanti: Rime* published in Genoa at Pound's expense.

May: Lectures on Cavalcanti in Palazzo Vecchio, Florence, as part of 'Settimana di Cultura'. (Joyce had declined the invitation and suggested Pound as alternative speaker.) Giovanni Scheiwiller publishes in Milan *Profile: An Anthology* ('A collection of poems which have stuck in my memory, and which may possibly define their epoch' – Pound).

June: Begins collaboration (1932–40) with London paper *New English Weekly*.

August 13: Mario Praz reviews Pound's *Cavalcanti Rime* for the national daily *La Stampa*, finding little to praise and much to amuse.

August 20: First issue of *Supplemento Letterario* of Rapallo weekly *Il Mare*, edited by Pound and Gino Saviotti (until March 18, 1933); it includes Olga's account of meeting in Rapallo between Pound and Ford Madox Ford (reprinted in *Pavannes and Divagations*).

December 21: *Le fiamme nere*, film-script by Pound and F. Ferruccio Cerio on Mussolini's March on Rome, privately published in Rapallo.

1933

January 30: Interview with Mussolini in Rome.

March 21–31: Lectures on poetry and economics at Università Bocconi, Milan.

June 26–28: Organizes 'Settimana Mozartiana' in Rapallo. Yeats briefly visits, finds Pound much changed and obsessed by economics and politics. Among guests at this time is US poet Louis Zukofsky.

Summer: In Siena with Olga, who works (1933–61) as secretary to Count Guido Chigi Saracini and the Accademia Chigiana. Later joins Olga and Mary in Venice.

October 10: First concert season ('Inverno Musicale'), organized by Pound for 'Amici del Tigullio', opens in 'Gran Sala del Municipio', Rapallo. Performances by Gerhart Münch, Olga Rudge, Luigi Sansoni, and others.

ABC of Economics. ABC of Reading. Make It New.

1934

Fall: Visits Venice Biennale. Comments on 'pore ole Marinetti' and American and French pavilions in a letter to *New English Weekly*, May 30, 1935.

October: James Laughlin, future publisher of New Directions, visits
    Rapallo.
Eleven New Cantos XXXI–XLI (Jefferson – Nuevo Mundo).

1935
July: In Gais (Tirol), Wörgl and Salzburg with Olga and Laughlin.
August: Meets Venetian critics Carlo Izzo and Aldo Camerino. In
    November sends Carlo Izzo glosses on the Venetian references in
    canto 3.
Social Credit: An Impact. Jefferson and/or Mussolini.

1936
April: 'Ore di studio' ('Hours of Study') devoted to Vivaldi as part of
    programme of 'Amici del Tigullio'.
May 2: Proposes in *Mare* that Rapallo become an 'International
    Center of Culture', catering to 'students of outstanding promise',
    and staffed by the *Mare* people.

1937
February 18: New Hungarian Quartet performs Bartok and Haydn
    in Rapallo.
March–April: Concerts of Vivaldi and others given by Rudge and
    Münch.
Polite Essays. The Fifth Decad of Cantos (Siena – The Leopoldine Reforms).

1938
January 21: Second Rapallo concert of New Hungarian Quartet; in
    February Rudge, Sansoni and Renata Borgatti play Purcell sonatas.
October 3: Mother-in-law Olivia Shakespear dies; travels to London
    to dispose of her belongings.

1939
January 4: Meets George Santayana in Rome.
March: Rapallo Mozart concerts.
April 13–June: Travels to US; visits New York, Washington, and
    Cambridge, Mass. Receives honorary doctorate from Hamilton
    College.
May: Begins collaboration (1939–42) with *Meridiano di Roma*, widely
    circulated cultural weekly edited by Cornelio Di Marzio.

September 6–21: 'Vivaldi Week' at Accademia Chigiana, Siena.

1940

February: *Cantos LII–LXXI* (*China – John Adams*). Writes in Dorothy's copy: 'To build up the city of Dioce . . . Whose terraces are the colour of stars'.

June 10: Italy declares war against France and England.

September: Attempts unsuccessfully to return to US.

1941

January: Begins broadcasts from Rome Radio.

June–July: Translates Enrico Pea's novella *Moscardino*.

1942

January 29: Resumes broadcasts, which he had interrupted after Pearl Harbor.

February 25: Homer Pound dies in Rapallo.

Confucio: *Studio integrale. Carta da visita.*

1943

July 24: Mussolini demoted by Grand Council of Fascism, and arrested on orders of King Victor Emmanuel III.

July 26: Pound indicted for treason by US Federal Grand Jury.

August 4: Writes letter in his defence to Attorney General Francis Biddle.

September 8: Armistice between Italy and Allies announced. German army occupies northern Italy.

September 10: Leaves Rome on foot and travels north by various means reuniting with daughter Mary in Gais, South Tyrol.

September 12: Pound's last contribution to *Meridiano di Roma*.

September 23: Proclamation in Northern Italy of Italian Social Republic, led by Mussolini under German tutelage.

November: Begins writing (1943–45) for fortnightly *Il Popolo di Alessandria*, organ of the Republican Fascist Party edited by Gian Gaetano Cabella.

1944

May: The Rapallo seafront is militarized. The Pounds move in with Olga at Sant'Ambrogio.

December 2: Marinetti, returned from the Russian front, dies in Bellagio. Pound at work on an Italian canto (72) in which he imagines a conversation with Marinetti's ghost.

Publishes Italian pamphlets: *L'America, Roosevelt e le cause della guerra presente*; *Oro e lavoro*; *Introduzione alla natura economica degli S.U.A.*; *Orientamenti* (a collection of articles from *Meridiano di Roma*); *Jefferson e Mussolini*.

1945

January 15 and February 1: Two Italian cantos (part of 72 and all of 73) appear in *Marina Repubblicana*, a fugitive paper edited by a friend, Admiral Ubaldo degli Uberti.

Chiung Iung: L'asse che non vacilla.

May 2: American troops in Rapallo.

May 3: Pound arrested in Sant'Ambrogio by two partisans and taken to Zoagli; thence, with Olga, to Chiavari headquarters. Asks to be handed over to American troops in Lavagna and is driven to US Counter Intelligence Center in Via Fieschi, 6, Genoa. Olga remains with him until May 7. US Intelligence officers visit Sant'Ambrogio and confiscate papers. While in Genoa has access to typewriter and translates *Studio integrale* as *The Great Learning*.

May 24: Transferred to US Disciplinary Training Center in Metato, north of Pisa. Writes (July–November) the *Pisan Cantos* (74–84).

November 16–18: Taken from Pisa to Rome and flown to Washington.

November 19: Appears before Chief Judge Bolitha J. Laws.

November 26: First hearing in court.

December 4: Transferred 'for observation' to Gallinger Hospital, as requested by Julien Cornell, counsel for defence.

December 14: Psychiatrists declare Pound 'insane and mentally unfit for trial'.

December 24: Motion for bail denied. Committed to St Elizabeths Hospital.

1946

February 13: New hearing confirms insanity.

July: Dorothy arrives in Washington.

September: Part of canto 80 appears in *Poetry*. Cantos 77 and 84 published in other journals.

October: Mary marries Boris de Rachewiltz.

1947

Confucius: The Unwobbling Pivot & The Great Digest published by New Directions.

Birth of grandson Siegfried Walter de Rachewiltz.

1948

January: Olga issues in Siena *If This Be Treason*, pamphlet containing six wartime broadcasts.

July 30: *The Pisan Cantos* published by New Directions.

October: Rapallo mayor and townspeople sign a statement declaring that Pound never participated in Fascist gatherings and 'anti-Semitic acts'.

1949

February 20: *Pisan Cantos* awarded Bollingen Prize for poetry by Library of Congress.

1950

Birth of grand-daughter Patrizia de Rachewiltz.

Letters 1907–1941, preface by Mark Van Doren. *Patria Mia.*

1951

Confucian Analects published in Square $ Series, series of pamphlets chosen by Pound (Ernest Fenollosa, Louis Agassiz, Alexander Del Mar, Thomas Hart Benton).

1952

Artist Sheri Martinelli (1918–96) visits Pound and becomes a protégée.

1953

The Translations, introduction by Hugh Kenner.

1954

Literary Essays, edited with an introduction by T. S. Eliot. *The Classic Anthology Defined by Confucius* (Harvard UP).

October 31: *Il Mare* prints a letter from Eliot, dated October 27,

stating that he hopes he will again meet Pound in Rapallo.
Writes short pieces for the Melbourne *New Times* (1954–57).

1955

September: *Section: Rock-Drill 85–95 de los Cantares* published by
 Vanni Scheiwiller in Milan.
*Ezra Pound: A Collection of Essays Edited by Peter Russell to Be Presented
 to Ezra Pound on His Seventieth Birthday.*

1956

February: *La Martinelli*, a booklet of reproductions with introduction
 by Pound, issued by Scheiwiller.
October: Contributes items to little magazine *Edge* (1956–57), edited
 by Noel Stock in Melbourne.
Genoa journal *Nuova Corrente* devotes double issue to 'Pound Sympo-
 sium'; Elizabeth Bishop contributes poem 'Visits to St Elizabeths'.
November: *Sophokles: Women of Trachis.*

1958

March 7: In Küsnacht (Zürich), H.D. begins notes posthumously
 published as *End to Torment: A Memoir of Ezra Pound* (1979).
April 18: Pound's indictment dismissed in District Court by Judge
 Laws.
May 7: Discharged from St Elizabeths in custody of Dorothy.
June: Makes Caedmon recordings of cantos and poems in Wash-
 ington. Visits Philadelphia and William Carlos Williams.
30 June: Sails from New York on *Cristoforo Colombo*, accompanied
 by Dorothy and Marcella Spann, 'a young woman who had first
 visited St Elizabeths in 1956 and was helping Pound to compile
 an anthology' (Noel Stock).
July 10: Arrives Genoa and, after revisiting Rapallo, goes on to Verona
 and Brunnenburg (Tirolo di Merano), residing with Mary and
 Boris de Rachewiltz.

1959

January: Back in Rapallo at Hotel Italia.
Summer: Rents apartment in Rapallo, works on new cantos (110–
 116).
September: Marcella Spann sails for US. In October Ezra and

Dorothy leave Rapallo apartment for Brunnenburg.
Thrones 96–109 de los Cantares. Versi prosaici.

1960

March: In Rome as houseguest of a friend; is interviewed for *Paris Review*. Increasingly exhausted and despondent.
Impact: Essays on Ignorance and the Decline of American Civilization, edited by Noel Stock.

1961

Hospitalized in Merano. Mary's Italian translation of *XXX Cantos* published.

1962

April: Returns to Sant'Ambrogio with Olga. From now on lives with Olga in Rapallo and Venice.
May 30–July 23: Seriously ill, is hospitalized and has operation in Rapallo. Regains strength but remains depressive and silent.
Receives award from Academy of American Poets.

1963

May 4–July 14: Readmitted to Rapallo clinic, has operation in late May.

1964

Confucius to Cummings: An Anthology of Poetry, edited by Pound and Spann.

1965

February 4: Attends T. S. Eliot memorial service, Westminster Abbey. Brief visit to Dublin and Mrs Yeats.
July 14–17: A ballet version of *Le Testament*, arranged by Gian Carlo Menotti, is produced at Spoleto Festival. Gives readings at Festival.
October–November: In Paris for his eightieth birthday, invited by magazine *L'Herne*, which devotes two volumes to his work. Travels in Greece (Athens, Delphi), accompanied by George Seferis.

1966

March 11–April 10: Hospitalized for depression in Neurological

Clinic, University of Genoa. Treatment brings little improvement.

1967
Autumn: Allen Ginsberg visits in Rapallo and Venice. Vanni Ronsis-
valle produces for RAI (Italian state television) *An Hour with Ezra
Pound*, which includes interview conducted by Pier Paolo Pasolini.

1969
April: *Drafts & Fragments of Cantos CX–CXVI.*
June 4–19: Brief trip to US (New York, Clinton, Philadelphia). Meets
Valerie Eliot in New York Public Library to review the recovered
Waste Land manuscripts.

1972
November 1: Dies in Venice.

I

Three Cantos

London, 1917

I

Hang it all, there can be but one *Sordello!*
But say I want to, say I take your whole bag of tricks,
Let in your quirks and tweeks, and say the thing's an art-form,
Your *Sordello*, and that the modern world
Needs such a rag-bag to stuff all its thought in;
Say that I dump my catch, shiny and silvery
As fresh sardines flapping and slipping on the marginal cobbles?
(I stand before the booth, the speech; but the truth
Is inside this discourse – this booth is full of the marrow of wisdom.)
Give up th' intaglio method.
                                        Tower by tower
Red-brown the rounded bases, and the plan
Follows the builder's whim. Beaucaire's slim gray
Leaps from the stubby base of Altaforte –
Mohammed's windows, for the Alcazar
Has such a garden, split by a tame small stream.
The moat is ten yards wide, the inner court-yard
Half a-swim with mire.
Trunk hose?
                There are not. The rough men swarm out
In robes that are half Roman, half like the Knave of Hearts;
And I discern your story:
                                Peire Cardinal
Was half forerunner of Dante. Arnaut's that trick
Of the unfinished address,
And half your dates are out, you mix your eras;
For that great font Sordello sat beside –

'Tis an immortal passage, but the font? –
Is some two centuries outside the picture.
Does it matter?

      Not in the least. Ghosts move about me
Patched with histories. You had your business:
To set out so much thought, so much emotion;
To paint, more real than any dead Sordello,
The half or third of your intensest life
And call that third *Sordello;*
And you'll say, 'No, not your life,
He never showed himself.'
Is't worth the evasion, what were the use
Of setting figures up and breathing life upon them,
Were 't not *our* life, your life, my life, extended?
I walk Verona. (I am here in England.)
I see Can Grande. (Can see whom you will.)

      You had one whole man?
And I have many fragments, less worth? Less worth?
Ah, had you quite my age, quite such a beastly and cantankerous age?
You had some basis, had some set belief.
Am I let preach? Has it a place in music?

      I walk the airy street,
See the small cobbles flare with the poppy spoil.
'Tis your 'great day', the Corpus Domini,
And all my chosen and peninsular village
Has made one glorious blaze of all its lanes –
Oh, before I was up – with poppy flowers.
Mid-June: some old god eats the smoke, 'tis not the saints;
And up and out to the half-ruined chapel –
Not the old place at the height of the rocks,
But that splay, barn-like church the Renaissance
Had never quite got into trim again.
As well begin here. Began our Catullus:
'Home to sweet rest, and to the waves' deep laughter',
The laugh they wake amid the border rushes.
This is our home, the trees are full of laughter,
And the storms laugh loud, breaking the riven waves
On 'north-most rocks'; and here the sunlight

Glints on the shaken waters, and the rain
Comes forth with delicate tread, walking from Isola Garda –
            Lo soleils plovil,
As Arnaut had it in th' inextricable song.
The very sun rains and a spatter of fire
Darts from the 'Lydian' ripples; *'lacus undae',* as Catullus, *'Lydiae',*
And the place is full of spirits.
Not *lemures,* not dark and shadowy ghosts,
But the ancient living, wood-white,
Smooth as the inner bark, and firm of aspect,
And all agleam with colours – no, not agleam,
But coloured like the lake and like the olive leaves,
Glaukopos, clothed like the poppies, wearing golden greaves,
Light on the air.
Are they Etruscan gods?
The air is solid sunlight, *apricus,*
Sun-fed we dwell there (we in England now);
It's your way of talk, we can be where we will be,
Sirmio serves my will better than your Asolo
Which I have never seen.
                        Your 'palace step'?
My stone seat was the Dogana's curb,
And there were not 'those girls', there was one flare, one face.
'Twas all I ever saw, but it was real.... .
And I can no more say what shape it was ...
But she was young, too young.
                        True, it was Venice,
And at Florian's and under the north arcade
I have seen other faces, and had my rolls for breakfast, for that matter;
So, for what it's worth, I have the background.
            And you had a background,
Watched 'the soul', Sordello's soul,
And saw it lap up life, and swell and burst –
'Into the empyrean?'
So you worked out new form, the meditative,
Semi-dramatic, semi-epic story,
And we will say: What's left for me to do?
Whom shall I conjure up; who's my Sordello,
My pre-Daun Chaucer, pre-Boccacio,

As you have done pre-Dante?
Whom shall I hang my shimmering garment on;
Who wear my feathery mantle, *hagoromo;*
Whom set to dazzle the serious future ages?
Not Arnaut, not De Born, not Uc St. Circ who has writ out the stories.
Or shall I do your trick, the showman's booth, Bob Browning,
Turned at my will into the Agora,
Or into the old theatre at Arles,
And set the lot, my visions, to confounding
The wits that have survived your damn'd *Sordello?*
(Or sulk and leave the word to novelists?)
What a hodge-podge you have made there! –
Zanze and *swanzig,* of all opprobrious rhymes!
And you turn off whenever it suits your fancy,
Now at Verona, now with the early Christians,
Or now a-gabbling of the 'Tyrrhene whelk'.
'The lyre should animate but not mislead the pen' –
That's Wordsworth, Mr. Browning. (What a phrase! –
That lyre, that pen, that bleating sheep, Will Wordsworth!)
That should have taught you avoid speech figurative
          And set out your matter
As I do, in straight simple phrases:
          Gods float in the azure air,
Bright gods, and Tuscan, back before dew was shed,
It is a world like Puvis'?
                Never so pale, my friend,
'Tis the first light – not half light – Panisks
And oak-girls and the Maenads
Have all the wood. Our olive Sirmio
Lies in its burnished mirror, and the Mounts Balde and Riva
Are alive with song, and all the leaves are full of voices.
'Non è fuggito'.
          'It is not gone'. Metastasio
Is right – we have that world about us,
And the clouds bow above the lake, and there are folk upon them
Going their windy ways, moving by Riva,
By the western shore, far as Lonato,
And the water is full of silvery almond-white swimmers,
The silvery water glazes the up-turned nipple.

How shall we start hence, how begin the progress?
Pace naif Ficinus, say when Hotep-Hotep
Was a king in Egypt –
  When Atlas sat down with his astrolabe,
  He, brother to Prometheus, physicist –
      Say it was Moses' birth-year?
Exult with Shang in squatness? The sea-monster
Bulges the squarish bronzes.
(Confucius later taught the world good manners,
Started with himself, built out perfection.)
          With Egypt!
Daub out in blue of scarabs, and with that greeny turquoise?
Or with China, *O Virgilio mio,* and gray gradual steps
Lead up beneath flat sprays of heavy cedars,
Temple of teak wood, and the gilt-brown arches
Triple in tier, banners woven by wall,
Fine screens depicted, sea waves curled high,
Small boats with gods upon them,
Bright flame above the river! Kwannon
Footing a boat that's but one lotus petal,
With some proud four-spread genius
Leading along, one hand upraised for gladness,
Saying, "Tis she, his friend, the mighty goddess! Paean!
Sing hymns ye reeds,
        and all ye roots and herons and swans be glad,
Ye gardens of the nymphs put forth your flowers'.
What have I of this life,
      Or even of Guido?
      Sweet lie! – Was I there truly?
Did I know Or San Michele?
      Let's believe it.
Believe the tomb he leapt was Julia Laeta's?
Friend, I do not even – when he led that street charge –
I do not even know which sword he'd with him.
Sweet lie, 'I lived!' Sweet lie, 'I lived beside him'.
And now it's all but truth and memory,
Dimmed only by the attritions of long time.

'But we forget not'.

　　　　　　　No, take it all for lies.
I have but smelt this life, a whiff of it –
The box of scented wood
Recalls cathedrals. And shall I claim;
Confuse my own phantastikon,
Or say the filmy shell that circumscribes me
Contains the actual sun;

　　　　　　　confuse the thing I see
With actual gods behind me?

　　　　　　　Are they gods behind me?
How many worlds we have! If Botticelli
Brings her ashore on that great cockle-shell –
His Venus (Simonetta?),
And Spring and Aufidus fill all the air
With their clear-outlined blossoms?
World enough. Behold, I say, she comes
'Apparelled like the spring, Graces her subjects',
(That's from *Pericles*).
Oh, we have worlds enough, and brave *décors*,
And from these like we guess a soul for man
And build him full of aery populations.
Mantegna a sterner line, and the new world about us:
Barred lights, great flares, new form, Picasso or Lewis.
If for a year man write to paint, and not to music –
O Casella!

II

Leave Casella.
Send out your thought upon the Mantuan palace –
Drear waste, great halls,
Silk tatters still in the frame, Gonzaga's splendour
Alight with phantoms! What have we of them,
Or much or little?
Where do we come upon the ancient people?
'All that I know is that a certain star' –
All that I know of one, Joios, Tolosan,
Is that in middle May, going along
A scarce discerned path, turning aside,
In level poplar lands, he found a flower, and wept.
'Y a la primera flor', he wrote,
'Qu'ieu trobei, tornei em plor'.
There's the one stave, and all the rest forgotten.
I've lost the copy I had of it in Paris,
Out of the blue and gilded manuscript
Decked out with Couci's rabbits,
And the pictures, twined with the capitals,
Purporting to be Arnaut and the authors.
Joios we have. By such a margent stream,
He strayed in the field, wept for a flare of colour,
When Coeur de Lion was before Chalus.
Or there's En Arnaut's score of songs, two tunes;
The rose-leaf casts her dew on the ringing glass,
Dolmetsch will build our age in witching music.
Viols da Gamba, tabors, tympanons:

'Yin-yo laps in the reeds, my guest departs,
The maple leaves blot up their shadows,
The sky is full of autumn,
We drink our parting in saki.
Out of the night comes troubling lute music,
And we cry out, asking the singer's name,
And get this answer:
                    "Many a one
Brought me rich presents; my hair was full of jade,
And my slashed skirts, drenched in expensive dyes,
Were dipped in crimson, sprinkled with rare wines.
I was well taught my arts at Ga-ma-rio,
And then one year I faded out and married".
The lute-bowl hid her face.
                              'We heard her weeping'.

    Society, her sparrows, Venus' sparrows, and Catullus
Hung on the phrase (played with it as Mallarmé
Played for a fan, *Rêveuse pour que je plonge'*);
Wrote out his crib from Sappho:
'God's peer that man is in my sight –
Yea, and the very gods are under him,
Who sits opposite thee, facing thee, near thee,
Gazing his fill and hearing thee,
And thou smilest. Woe to me, with
Quenched senses, for when I look upon thee, Lesbia,
There is nothing above me
And my tongue is heavy, and along my veins
Runs the slow fire, and resonant
Thunders surge in behind my ears,
And the night is thrust down upon me'.

    That was the way of love, *flamma dimanat.*
And in a year, 'I love her as a father';
And scarce a year, 'Your words are written in water';
And in ten moons, *'Caelius, Lesbia illa –*
That Lesbia, Caelius, our Lesbia, that Lesbia
Whom Catullus once loved more
Than his own soul and all his friends,

Is now the drab of every lousy Roman'.
So much for him who puts his trust in woman.
So the murk opens.
                              Dordoigne! When I was there,
There came a centaur, spying the land,
And there were nymphs behind him.
Or going on the road by Salisbury
Procession on procession –
For that road was full of peoples,
Ancient in various days, long years between them.
Ply over ply of life still wraps the earth here.
Catch at Dordoigne.
                              Viscount St. Antoni
In the warm damp of spring,
Feeling the night air full of subtle hands,
Plucks at a viol, singing:
                              'As the rose –
Si com, si com' – they all begin *'si com'*.
'For as the rose in trellis
Winds in and through and over,
So is your beauty in my heart, that is bound through and over.
So lay Queen Venus in her house of glass,
The pool of worth thou art,
                              Flood-land of pleasure'.
  But the Viscount Pena
Went making war into an hostile country
Where he was wounded:
'The news held him dead'.
St. Antoni in favour, and the lady
Ready to hold his hands –
This last report upset the whole convention.
She rushes off to church, sets up a gross of candles,
Pays masses for the soul of Viscount Pena.

  Thus St. Circ has the story:
'That sire Raimon Jordans, of land near Caortz,
Lord of St. Antoni, loved this Viscountess of Pena
"Gentle" and "highly prized".
And he was good at arms and *bos trobaire*,

And they were taken with love beyond all measure',
And then her husband was reported dead,
'And at this news she had great grief and sorrow',
And gave the church such wax for his recovery,
That he recovered, and
'At this news she had great grief and teen',
And fell to moping, dismissed St. Antoni;
'Thus was there more than one in deep distress'.

So ends that novel. And the blue Dordoigne
Stretches between white cliffs,
Pale as the background of a Leonardo.
'As rose in trellis, that is bound over and over',
A wasted song?
                    No Elis, Lady of Montfort,
Wife of William à Gordon, heard of the song,
Sent him her mild advances.
                              Gordon? Or Gourdon
Juts into the sky
                    Like a thin spire,
Blue night's pulled down around it
Like tent flaps, or sails close hauled. When I was there,
La noche de San Juan, a score of players
Were walking about the streets in masquerade,
With pikes and paper helmets, and the booths,
Were scattered align, the rag ends of the fair.
False arms! True arms? You think a tale of lances …
A flood of people storming about Spain!
                              My cid rode up to Burgos,
Up to the studded gate between two towers,
Beat with his lance butt.
                          A girl child of nine,
Comes to a little shrine-like platform in the wall,
Lisps out the words, a-whisper, the King's writ:
'Let no man speak to Diaz or give him help or food
On pain of death, his eyes torn out,
His heart upon a pike, his goods sequestered'.
He from Bivar, cleaned out,
From empty perches of dispersed hawks,

From empty presses,
Came riding with his company up the great hill –
'Afe Minaya!' –
                    to Burgos in the spring,
And thence to fighting, to down-throw of Moors,
And to Valencia rode he, by the beard! –
Muy velida.
                    Of onrush of lances,
Of splintered staves, riven and broken casques,
Dismantled castles, of painted shields split up,
Blazons hacked off, piled men and bloody rivers;
Then 'sombre light upon reflecting armor'
And portents in the wind, when De las Nieblas
Set out to sea-fight,
'Y dar neuva lumbre las armas y hierros'.
Full many a fathomed sea-change in the eyes
That sought with him the salt sea victories.
Another gate?
                    And Kumasaka's ghost come back to tell
The honour of the youth who'd slain him.
Another gate.
                    The kernelled walls of Toro, *las almenas;*
Afield, a king come in an unjust cause.
Atween the chinks aloft flashes the armored figure,
Muy linda, a woman, Helen, a star,
Lights the king's features ...
                              'No use, my liege –
She is your highness' sister', breaks in Ancures;
'Mal fuego s'enciende!'
Such are the gestes of war 'told over and over'.
And Ignez?
                    Was a queen's tire-woman,
Court sinecure, the court of Portugal;
And the young prince loved her – Pedro,
Later called the cruel. And other courtiers were jealous.
Two of them stabbed her with the king's connivance,
And he, the prince, kept quiet a space of years –
                    Uncommon the quiet.
And he came to reign, and had his will upon the dagger-players,

And held his court, a wedding ceremonial –
He and her dug-up corpse in cerements
Crowned with the crown and splendour of Portugal.
A quiet evening and a decorous procession;
Who winked at murder kisses the dead hand,
Does leal homage,
'Que depois de ser morta foy Rainha'.
Dig up Camoens, hear out his resonant bombast:
           'That among the flowers,
As once was Proserpine,
Gatheredst thy soul's light fruit and every blindness,
Thy Enna the flary mead-land of Mondego,
Long art thou sung by maidens in Mondego'.
What have we now of her, his *'linda Ignez'*?
Houtmans in jail for debt in Lisbon – how long after? –
Contrives a company, the Dutch eat Portugal,
Follow her ship's tracks, Roemer Vischer's daughters,
Talking some Greek, dally with glass engraving;
Vondel, the Eglantine, Dutch Renaissance –
The old tale out of fashion, daggers gone;
And Gaby wears Braganza on her throat –
Commuted, say, another public pearl
Tied to a public gullet. Ah, *mon rêve*,
It happened; and now go think –
Another crown, thrown to another dancer, brings you to modern times?

    I knew a man, but where 'twas is no matter:
Born on a farm, he hankered after painting;
His father kept him at work;
No luck – he married and got four sons;
Three died, the fourth he sent to Paris –
Ten years of Julian's and the ateliers,
Ten years of life, his pictures in the salons,
Name coming in the press.
                    And when I knew him,
Back once again, in middle Indiana,
Acting as usher in the theatre,
Painting the local drug-shop and soda bars,
The local doctor's fancy for the mantel-piece;

Sheep – jabbing the wool upon their flea-bit backs –
The local doctor's ewe-ish pastoral;
Adoring Puvis, giving his family back
What they had spent for him, talking Italian cities,
Local excellence at Perugia,

                          dreaming his renaissance,

Take my Sordello!

III

Another's a half-cracked fellow – John Heydon,
Worker of miracles, dealer in levitation,
In thoughts upon pure form, in alchemy,
Seer of pretty visions ('servant of God and secretary of nature');
Full of a plaintive charm, like Botticelli's,
With half-transparent forms, lacking the vigor of gods.
Thus Heydon, in a trance, at Bulverton,
Had such a sight:
Decked all in green, with sleeves of yellow silk
Slit to the elbow, slashed with various purples.
Her eyes were green as glass, her foot was leaf-like.
She was adorned with choicest emeralds,
And promised him the way of holy wisdom.
'Pretty green bank', began the half-lost poem.
Take the old way, say I met John Heydon,
Sought out the place,
Lay on the bank, was 'plungèd deep in swevyn';
And saw the company – Layamon, Chaucer –
Pass each in his appropriate robes;
Conversed with each, observed the varying fashion.
And then comes Heydon.
                              'I have seen John Heydon'.
Let us hear John Heydon!
                              '*Omniformis*
Omnis intellectus est' – thus he begins, by spouting half of Psellus.
(Then comes a note, my assiduous commentator:
Not Psellus *De Daemonibus*, but Porphyry's *Chances*,

In the thirteenth chapter, that 'every intellect is omniform'.)
Magnifico Lorenzo used the dodge,
Says that he met Ficino
In some Wordsworthian, false-pastoral manner,
And that they walked along, stopped at a well-head,
And heard deep platitudes about contentment
From some old codger with an endless beard.
'A daemon is not a particular intellect,
But is a substance differed from intellect',
Breaks in Ficino,
'Placed in the latitude or locus of souls' –
That's out of Proclus, take your pick of them.
Valla, more earth and sounder rhetoric –
Prefacing praise to his Pope Nicholas:
'A man of parts, skilled in the subtlest sciences;
A patron of the arts, of poetry; and of a fine discernment'.
Then comes a catalogue, his jewels of conversation.
No, you've not read your *Elegantiae* –
A dull book? – shook the church.
The prefaces, cut clear and hard:
'Know then the Roman speech, a sacrament',
Spread for the nations, eucharist of wisdom,
Bread of the liberal arts.

           Ha! Sir Blancatz,
Sordello would have your heart to give to all the princes;
Valla, the heart of Rome,
Sustaining speech, set out before the people.
'Nec bonus Christianus ac bonus
               Tullianus'.
Marius, Du Bellay, wept for the buildings,
Baldassar Castiglione saw Raphael
'Lead back the soul into its dead, waste dwelling',
Corpore laniato; and Lorenzo Valla,
'Broken in middle life? bent to submission? –
Took a fat living from the Papacy'
(That's in Villari, but Burckhardt's statement is different) –
'More than the Roman city, the Roman speech'
(Holds fast its part among the ever-living).
'Not by the eagles only was Rome measured'.

'Wherever the Roman speech was, there was Rome',
Wherever the speech crept, there was mastery
Spoke with the law's voice while your Greek logicians …
More Greeks than one! Doughty's 'divine Homeros'
Came before sophistry. Justinopolitan
Uncatalogued Andreas Divus,
Gave him in Latin, 1538 in my edition, the rest uncertain,
Caught up his cadence, word and syllable:
'Down to the ships we went, set mast and sail,
Black keel and beasts for bloody sacrifice,
Weeping we went'.
I've strained my ear for *-ensa, -ombra,* and *-ensa*
And cracked my wit on delicate canzoni –
            Here's but rough meaning:
'And then went down to the ship, set keel to breakers,
Forth on the godly sea;
We set up mast and sail on the swarthy ship,
Sheep bore we aboard her, and our bodies also
Heavy with weeping. And winds from sternward
Bore us out onward with bellying canvas –
Circe's this craft, the trim-coifed goddess.
Then sat we amidships, wind jamming the tiller.
Thus with stretched sail
            We went over sea till day's end:
Sun to his slumber, shadows o'er all the ocean.
Came we then to the bounds of deepest water,
To the Kimmerian lands and peopled cities
Covered with close-webbed mist, unpiercèd ever
With glitter of sun-rays,
Nor with stars stretched, nor looking back from heaven,
Swartest night stretched over wretched men there.
Thither we in that ship, unladed sheep there,
The ocean flowing backward, came we through to the place
Aforesaid by Circe.
Here did they rites, Perimedes and Eurylochus,
And drawing sword from my hip
I dug the ell-square pitkin, poured we libations unto each the dead,
First mead and then sweet wine,
Water mixed with white flour.

Then prayed I many a prayer to the sickly death's-heads
As set in Ithaca, sterile bulls of the best,
For sacrifice, heaping the pyre with goods.
Sheep, to Tiresias only,
Black, and a bell sheep;
Dark blood flowed in the fosse.
Souls out of Erebus, cadaverous dead
Of brides, of youths, and of many passing old,
Virgins tender, souls stained with recent tears,
Many men mauled with bronze lance-heads,
Battle spoil, bearing yet dreary arms:
These many crowded about me,
With shouting, pallor upon me, cried to my men for more beasts;
Slaughtered the herds – sheep slain of bronze,
Poured ointment, cried to the gods,
To Pluto the strong, and praised Proserpine.
Unsheathed the narrow steel,
I sat to keep off the impetuous, impotent dead
Till I should hear Tiresias.
But first Elpenor came, our friend Elpenor,
Unburied, cast on the wide earth –
Limbs that we left in the house of Circe,
Unwept, unwrapped in sepulchre, since toils urged other,
Pitiful spirit – and I cried in hurried speech:
"Elpenor, how art thou come to this dark coast?
Cam'st thou afoot, outstripping seamen?" And he in heavy speech:
"Ill fate and abundant wine! I slept in Circe's ingle,
Going down the long ladder unguarded, I fell against the buttress,
Shattered the nape-nerve, the soul sought Avernus.
But thou, O King, I bid remember me, unwept, unburied!
Heap up mine arms, be tomb by the sea-board, and inscribed,
A man of no fortune and with a name to come;
And set my oar up, that I swung 'mid fellows".
Came then another ghost, whom I beat off, Anticlea,
And then Tiresias, Theban,
Holding his golden wand, knew me and spoke first:
"Man of ill hour, why come a second time,
Leaving the sunlight, facing the sunless dead and this joyless region?
Stand from the fosse, move back, leave me my bloody bever,

And I will speak you true speeches".
                                    And I stepped back,
Sheathing the yellow sword. Dark blood he drank then
And spoke: "Lustrous Odysseus, shalt
Return through spiteful Neptune, over dark seas,
Lose all companions". Foretold me the ways and the signs.
Came then Anticlea, to whom I answered:
"Fate drives me on through these deeps; I sought Tiresias".
I told her news of Troy, and thrice her shadow
        Faded in my embrace.
Then had I news of many faded women –
Tyro, Alcmena, Chloris –
Heard out their tales by that dark fosse, and sailed
By sirens and thence outward and away,
And unto Circe buried Elpenor's corpse'.

Lie quiet, Divus.
                    In Officina Wechli, Paris,
M. D. three X's, Eight, with Aldus on the Frogs,
And a certain Cretan's
                    Hymni Deorum:
(The thin clear Tuscan stuff
    Gives way before the florid mellow phrase.)
Take we the Goddess, Venus:
                    Venerandam,
Auream coronam habentem, pulchram,
Cypri munimenta sortita est, maritime,
Light on the foam, breathed on by zephyrs,
And air-tending hours. Mirthful, *orichalci,* with golden
Girdles and breast bands.
                    Thou with dark eye-lids,
Bearing the golden bough of Argicida.

IV

'What do I mean by all this clattering rumble?'
Bewildered reader, what is the poet's business?
To fill up chaos, populate solitudes, multiply images
Or streak the barren way to paradise
        (Here was the renaissance)
Band out fine colours, fill the void with stars
And make each star a nest of noble voices.
Let undines hear me, and in cool streams   *faut un*
Redeck the muses' gardens, green herbs and cress   *bois aux*
And water-drinking flowers . . . .   *rossignols*
Rumble again? 'What are the muses' gardens?'
Oh, take a heaven you know, and make the starry wood
Sound like a wood well filled with nightingales,
And call lights 'souls',
And say: The lights ascending . . . like a covey of partridges.
Thus much I saw above me, and beneath, looking into the water,
Beheld the turret as a pillar of fire reflected,
And thence to God,
To the ineffable, *trashumanar non si potria per verba.*

The soul starts with itself, builds out perfection,
Confucius, Dante.
                        Or the best man killed in France,
Struck by a Prussian bullet at St Vaast
With just enough cut stone left here behind him
To show a new way to the kindred arts,
Laying a method, quite outside his art,

Vortex, dispersal, throw it at history.

Say that the prose is life, scooped out of time,
A bristling node ... and I am all too plain,
Too full of footnotes, too careful to tell you
The how and why of my meaning 'here was the renaissance',
Venus intaglio'd in the papal gem.
Lewis with simpler means
Catches the age, his Timon,
Throws our few years onto a score of pasteboards,
Says all our conflict, edgey, epigrammatic,
This Timon lived in Greece, and loved the people,
And gave high feasts, and dug his rabbit burrow.

'And Ka-hu churned the sea,
Churning the ocean, using the moon for a churn-stick.'

When you find that feminine contact
has no longer the richness
of Omakitsu's verses,
Know then, o man,
        that the Cytherean has turned from you,
                fugges!
When the smoke no longer
        hangs upon the lacquer,
When the night air no longer clings
        to your cuticle,
When the air has in it no
        mystery about her,
Know then that the days
        of your adolescence are ended
        fugaces, fugges, fugus

What's poetry?

       There is a castle set,

The Auvezere, or it's Dordoigne, chalk white and whiteish blue,

Or Goldring writes 'That night, the Loredan'

And the blue-black of Venice fills my mind

And the gilt rafters of the first floor rooms

       Show there above me all a-red, ablaze,

'I knew it first, and it was such a year,

When first I knew it there was such an air'

Or 'This night it will happen'. 'Further on'.

Or 'Down you go, a mile from Angouleme

And in an open field there are three steps

Grey stone, they wait, there is no yard behind them,

Only the stone piers that have held the gate'.

Or 'The red poppies seem to swim in glass'

That's Spain, your dusty France

       holds half the colour back,

Your temperate eyes . . .

              'Arles gray, what gray?

The church of St Trophime.'

II

Paris

1922–1935

And So shu stirred in the sea
              using the moon for a churn-stick.
Clots, blocks, islands of detached vision, colour amorphous,
Floating hills, long valleys of high rock-wall
Endless, detached, unending.
              Santa Theresa's nut,
Cosmos held in her fingers,
              e sen andava giù a capo chino,
Bending over his sphere, crystal, the ball of fire
A globed light held in the hands,
              the figure hooded and walking,
Sight within sphere of crystal.
              So shu stirred in the sea,
Dissatisfaction of chaos, inadequacy of arrangements,
At les Eyzies, nameless drawer of panther,
So I in narrow cave, secret scratched on a wall,
And the last reader, with handshake of departing sun
drifts from sorrowful horizon, patient thus far, now impatient
e tu lettor, with little candle long after,
have pushed past the ruined castle, past the underbrush
              tangled and netted
past the ant-hive, in narrow dark of the crevice
On the damp rock, is my panther, my aurochs scratched
              in obscurity,
Died thus, Po, Nai, Lun, Ak, and the guild of carvers

But glare azure, wall translucent above her

High flow over fork-tracked beaches
Sea living and turning, lithe water, flaked, clear as Poseidon,
And the twisted arms of the sea-god
                              Χαῖρε, γύναι, φιλότητι;
Bride of Neptunus,
                    and the soft sand, quiet,
and soothed with ripples, quassator terrae
          shaker and breaker of ships
of the strong arms, Ποσειδῶν, suitor of Tyro,
Quiet in the long nights; the sky deep with black-azure
And again the sand and the wave, again the vitreous darkness
                                        and hyaline

reach and embrace of waves
subsidence of waters Ποσειδῶν
shaker of earth, Τυρώ bride of the waters,
That Aeolidaus had for mistress, at the first flush of breasts,
          bride of the sea-god . . .

Bathing seabirds broad out their feathers,
          Ne maeg merigmod wyrdhe widhstondan . . .
                              Gone might of the seagod
Dark coast, no wall of wave's weight
high towers over Tyro
No crystal closeness to cover the sea-sward
No water's welter, weft over woman,
No cloth of brightness, no glitter of glass-wave,
Glints no small peak of wave,
                    greyness fore-gathered
Dark mist is murky, grey rock on meer's edge.

Age totters outward, old eyes toward ocean,
Seeing no men return,
                    no boats in offing,
Batter of waves on cliff,
                              salt-lick of dolphins,
Seal head in white-circled waters, seal-eye in slumber,
Sport of the young seal, the fearless swimmer's.

Sudden gift of the stranger   *Ghazel 1919*
Favour of unknown beauty
No ancient glory ever fades from the world

High halls with their splendid trappings
Hidden behind a mean wall
No high thought but hath some heart
                                        still for its hostel
No ancient glory ever fades from the world

Brows cut smoothe as if with a jade-wheel
Cool water of hill-lakes, water calm as the eyes

No ancient glory
                        ever fades from the world

So shu churrned in the sea
            using the moon for a churn-stick.
Glare-azure, translucent above her wall-wave
High over Tyro, high through the fork-tracked beaches
Living and turning water;
            water lithe, water flaked, swirl-wreathed
On the green-deep, deep clear as Poseidon
XAIRE TYRO, XAIRE PHILOTETI,
twisted arms of the sea-god,
            and the soft sand, sand then, quiet, quiet,
Smoothed with the ripples, quassator terrae,

POSEIDON breaker of ships.
Where then TYRO, sea-bride, now seabirds
bathing, broad out their feathers,
Ne mawg werigmod wyrdthe widhstondon,
Seal-head in white-swirled water,
Et dixit Acoetes:

Dido choked up with tears for dead Sicheus;
And the weeping Muse, weeping, widowed, and willing,
The weeping Muse
                    Mourns Homer,
Mourns the days of long song,
Mourns for the breath of the singers,
Winds stretching out, seas pulling to eastward,
Heaving breath of the oarsmen,
                    triremes under Cyprus,
The long course of the seas,
The words woven in wind-wrack,
                         salt spray over voices.
Tyro to shoreward lies lithe with Neptunus
And the glass-clear wave arches over them;
Seal sports in the spray-whited circles of cliff-wash,
Sleek head, daughter of Lir,
                    eyes of Picasso
Under black fur-hood, lithe daughter of Ocean

By the arena, you, Thomas amics, Galla Placidia, and the Roman.
inside it, the footlights, the clowns, dancers
performing dogs.
        As we had sat, three of us at Excideuil
over Borneil's old bake oven
                (hidden below in the cellarage)
... that was three years ago ...
              on the roman mound
level with the town spire.
                'e poi gli affina' for you.
Me swinging the burning head,
        peering into the crevices, uselessly.
           the act goes on,
I have sat here a thousand years, or
            forty-four thousand years
Here on this wooden chair,
           & your bitter Bonomelli is a worse red than Egypt's,
Things run, and run to the worse,
Ti, Galla's hypostasis, had herself better painted
        in grey stone, cut – intagliata
      the shadow faces in from the grove's edge.
yes a better red that sappy analine
        that soaks your yellow straw,
Ti and the Chinese empress. then,
      and the arena behind us
               all these sprouts in the loam,

The roman takes her form from the stones
                              more clearly,
(I have sat here, you know, for forty four thousand years)

The Byzantine disintegrates,
                              puts on Venetian clogs,
digs into your powdered past,
                              sniffs your soiled cuff lace,
At which time I?
                              was lifting sedan chairs, preparing the revolution
(in a brown fustian coat)
                              paying the bill,
for the Veronese 'banquet'.
                              & . . . never learning . .
hell, do we ever learn . . .

                    and she's buried in Ravenna,
lit by the alabaster panes,
                              yellow, sun yellow, in the gloom the gold
gathers the light against it,
                              Byzance
& the empires gone, slide to nothing here
              in the marsh drift,
Caesarea, gone, roof deep in the marsh,
                              between the town and Classe
Empires end in the marsh.

                    So the gate shuts.
Between the great phalloi of the temple,

                                        the winding path.
                    on mosaic walls, the souls,
gonads in organdy, rose-flakes in the arid darkness,
a wing exists for a moment and goes out,
              flame intermittent
an emerald lizard peers through the border grass
              & the white processional figures over him

III

Rapallo and Venice

1928–1937

the new shoots rise by the altar
        spread to the chancel
the new shoots – short rooted Adonis –
the bay is dotted with light –
        dotted with floating lanthorns
carmine – of colour
        hot blood colours the sea
        ἄδωνιν   ἄδωνιν
who shall carry the torch to [the caves]
shall the walls ruddy with flame
        with splendour –
& then beat his head against stone.

art thou 2 spans long to a woman
        seek not to surpass that
she hath a mind in her middle
therein is her comprehension
   [tota famam sexus]
beyond that she considers thee nonsense
thou art, by God, her nonsense –
nor will be by jactancy of her.
emptiness is her sky
        nor will she consider the constellations
but flowers
        she hath the grain's completeness
tears are her irrigation, her grain
art thou a span long or 2 spans

she looketh up feignedly – thus
               she seeketh her timing
& by her dost thou mount to the stars
in her is thy liberation
             thy rocket is to rise & to fall
wilt thou [travel] thine eye beam?
           so mayst thou
so mayst thou also travel alone
plucking first thy bough from her forest
She wd keep thy will
                   by always at udder
knowing no bit but the sword –
have it ready
       & μῶλυ the herb
                       keep that ready
aut in harum
         to the sty with the sailor lads
διογενής – Laertiade, goest thou

irritable and unstable
      is formed but to be destroyed
  recomposes
to be but once more decomposed. by day there is
starch in the leaf,
                      by night it escapeth away.

toward the cliffs at Macaud, witness a fisherman,
walked quite quietly together, and leapt . . .
      toward the clear height, the empyrean
with the bodies we found no papers . . .

valeurs, nom de dieu, the two arrow that
make three wounds . . . he thirty, and she about twenty three

in the clear light, of Var, the sun gone over meridian.
the sea clear, under the crag . . .

Helene la distrait, doing always two things at a time . . .
the cicada seeks shade in winter, for the sun then leaves
      him no quiet/ so he perches still, day by day . . .
in the quiet, avoiding Progne,
      hearing Philomela or mayhap asleep and unhearing.
But you wd. not know the sound of a hand loom
      or the noise of a man beating for olives . . .
            nor wd/ the gray stones of the paths
                speak in your presence. . .

But they are then called the twice born/ called
sometimes leopards;
when they have spent these years in the forest.
their mind is not shut in a box . . .
no longer shut in the skull
They say the road died in the forest.
that wd. be when no one passed by it.
Desire/ Goddess of Cythera; that was born in the sea marge/

when the winged sparks of an evening
flow under boughs, come to rest on the grass
under cypress, float between
high bough and the lower branch of the olive trees.
for the calm night, by St John's eve.
The long ridge rises out of the world,
till there are twin seas in the cloud;
and as it were Scilla's teeth under the headland;
the light from the far sea, rises over the headland.
Titular head, be Pu Yi.

But your wheat, kubanka, red Kharkov;
that you will sow in the plain land,
that you will sow in the far level country,
with no sea under your eaves;
with no grey of the branch, no light thrown and ret[o]rted
by the trees of good council,
green by the over leaf, and gray under . . . But your wheat that
Carleton brought out of Kharkov,
and for which he was never paid . . . in this world.
for this you will do your plowing. and give no thanks to the god.
Sitalkas will not walk in your harvest . . .
nor will the gift of healing be found there . . .
Nor will the lights float in your harbor
when they are weeping
'Adonin, Adonin'
'and I have tried to keep them from falling'

τὺ Διώνα

Καὶ Μοῖραι τ᾽Ἄδωνιν,

ἀνακλαίουσιν Ἄδωνιν

'Galileo' (vague voice under the trees) 'er'un i'norante
ed ha imbecilito il mondo'

'Spent yesterday drawing a grasshopper'

                              19 Aug. 1928

And To Fan pasted these things in a book,
scraps, tatters, of Tc'ihng Thsung lake,
went there, habit, a great lot of them went there
                    that would have been around 1750
drew, and then wrote their tanka.

Wild geese on the sand bar
Bullrushes, have burst into snow-tops
            as it were snow on their heads
Milky jade film covers it all
All thus covered with jade, a film of
                              whitish film
The water congeals, Sai Yin,
                    men of sai yin
are unhurried.

The boat there like a leaf,
Noise of fishermen landing,
one light under the awning,

Or:
     bell sounds under mist
with the wind moving toward one,
I know not if I am near or far from the peak,
But in a hollow of mountain

'From this grotto'
                        as H.J. has recorded
in slightly inaccurate manner
or at least without explaining the details
                        'Lord Byron'
A quarante ans et force ma gourme jecté
'Traversing the waters of the Thyrennian sea'
Both he and Swinburne good swimmers
            'to the further shore (Lerici) as of Hellespont
with peril of waves passed over'.

For the Seven Lakes, and by no man these verses
Rain, empty river, a voyage
From the frozen cloud: fire, heavy rain in the twilight
Under the felze (that is the cabin, or almost)
            one lantern
The reeds are heavy, the bamboos speak as if weeping.

For the autumn moon in these lakes
Hills rise against sunset

A dangle of fishermen's lanthorns
        & the rooks start their clatter
A light moves on the north sky line
A light moves on the south sky line,
        kids poking for shrimp
A fisherman sends the boy for his bottle,
They lie drinking and watching the cattails.
In seventeen sometime, came Tsing to these lakes.

And the hail sprouts a myriad tails in the
Canale Giudecca; a thousand cats plunging.
               gift of healing;
no fate but another's; Il Moro
via lactea, model dairy, DIGENES
          That the state by creating riches
          shd. thereby run into debt
This is infamy, this is Geryon
That the state in making a city, shd. run into debt to
privati, to Johnson and Bernstein, this is an infamy;
that you shd. send food abroad before feeding your people
this is Geryon, this is an infamy

        the tradition
is full of wrong things, dug canal from Benriu
they say for his pleasure, they say he sailed there with women
bringing the north and south together
and this canal goes still to TenShi

they may go north by interior waters
          in his time was Otsu
And Yodai killed an author from jealousy if his writings,
under taxes, for the conquest of Korea, under taxes
for the canal bill. Watching the dance that is still Hagoromo. . .
watching, heard that Gokan had fallen.

kei	men	ran	kei
kiu	man	man	kei

SHINES in the mind of heaven GOD
                         who made it
More than the sun in our eye.
                         Which statement
without application is now an affair for poltroons
Shines in the mind of heaven, statement dated, Guinicello,
                                    anno domini
       twelve hundred say seventy something
                  Shines
in the mind of heaven
God who made it, more than the sun,
        melt earth, burn air
let the light of the fire die,
        shines in the mind the Rightness,
falling the embers, involving the movement, stillness
over the glaze, a light
Time like a bed bug   cimex,   Time,
a centipede, scuttles under the door
        illusion? matter illusion? time rather!
and speaking of righteousness
        lacking the concrete example
Old Bob at the seance with the voice, say Gigadibs
Bloughram, Robert redivivus Browning
ectoplasmic R.B. like suds over a beer stein
and the mud said Guinicello
                  mud unchanged
the sun glares on it all day and the mud stays vile
MEN AI DE, in the spring time Rolando

colla coda aguzza
>   that you nears has befogged all text books

fifth element MUD said Napoleon,
ledt hoo vill rhun de harmies,
>   if I can gontroll the gredit
that passeth wall, and blunteth every sharp weapon
out of slime, belching smoke, Geryon,
>   slow circling, winged, viscous, slow moving
in nether air, ever descending,

>   Hath lost the sense of partaggio,
hath bartered birthright, contra natura,
give not to thy brother, ever descending,
into the greasy air, nether inferno,

>   this beast hath absorbed the lightning,
this beast spreadeth darkness.
under his shadow is quiet, cometh their stupor,
>   then death of the spirit.
>   a little light in that darkness,
greasy flame of dead gas flare
ever low descended, between his great wings
>   there is quiet
as is before thunder, a thick air
>   and a stifled silence
Fly sticks to agave

is burried the great financier, Lawvi or Levi
of Edinburg origin,
                              genius
after debts left by Louis Soleil
thus the ambassador, Morosini, in margin
with clarity to his city
                              (quote that law)

in which time Vivaldi was given or said to
                    to vertigo
which prevented his saying mass
which made him an impresario
composer with ballerine, or with a ballerina,
with troubles about rehearsals, as has happened,
with fuss over contracts, as haps and happened,
touring with a theatrical company, il prete rosso
the carrot topped sacerdote
    whom Bach barely improved on
as you like it
    in some ways, and in others open to question
        doceat, moveat, ut delectet
            Daladier greatly defamed.

while they were discussing the former possibility
          in came the gombeen men
USURA, thicker usura
XIXth siècle said Le Marquis
will be known as the usurers' century
          'The old Marquis' as she said to me
was distressed that they (people) would not
consider these subjects   Jalons de Route
privately printed
                    a profit to the bishops of Durham
between the metal and the face value
If a cavalry officer in that milieu
          quoting Destutt de Tracy in 1889 and
in the days of 'Coin' Harvey
there is after all a tradition
Mr Law (regii Galliae)
is burried under the floor of St Moses
sui cineres, sui generis
with the poodle dogs on the façade
          inscribed in a bit of paving
                              ◊ just inside the door

J. Law inglese on this rock
'shalt thou build Prudential
          and a great flock of holdings'
Morosini in proposito
                    QUOTE

I am serious, as a judge, I am serious
in St Moses church, that is in Venice
with the mouldly sheeplike façade

Lost sense of partaggio, of sharing, for fellowship
and therewith il ben del intellecto
          Cythera and Apollo
and between them the man with the bag
          the gombeen man
Sandro painting La Calomnia
while their eyes were diverted
          came that old serpent Usura
   the crawling belly, and sapped their foundations
          the 5th element MUD
5% of erosion, 60% of erosion
'in totality does not pay'
                              (Dexter Kimball)
or letter by letter, first a salt tax
then all the gabelle
          then all the imports
5% here and 5 there

with the face of a prelate
                    with solemnity and exactitude
          bleeding the people
in the nave of San Giorgio
          getting Teutonic taxes
to build an opera house for St Peter
'paradiso dei sarti' Tiziano for Bellini
as mind sank into belly
          design sank into fatness

phallos pharos mentis!
　　　belly bulge after 1527

In their pageantry and their pride they were 40
the young palukas, in their uniforms, the knuts of the party
and plump young marchese among them.
the secretaries, gerarchia,
received by the Duce,
and waiting more splendour.
('What does the working man pay for his veal
in your local market?'
no answer,
                    and thus they passed
out of history
          or the history of a nation.

'Das endlich eine wirklicheVerständigung
zwischen den Völkern erzielt wird'
                                    Hess, Königsberg 34
Yes! es die höchste Zeit ist.
       That hath the light of the Doer
as it were a form cleaving to it,
and from the possible, the receptive: intellectum adeptus
deo similis quodam modo
power, as it were, of the gods,
when thou hast thought all the thought,
felicity, then, contemplativa
: contemplatio / the thing there before thy mind

that thy mind shall pass into, to see then with its eye
       O grass my uncle, that art nowhere out of place
Es ist die höchste, das endlich, zwischen die Völkern, eine
Verständigung . . .
       light the first form in matter
that hath as it were form cleaving to it.
from the possible, intellectus adeptus /
       whether common hackle or wing'd fly   the young angler
should watch a skilled maker, having all the materials
strip hackle of the soft fibers, the dubbing
to be already properly coloured /
   you will make the body from the red fur of a squirrel,
red cock's hackle wrapped twice under the wings.
or wrap it three times,
from ten in the morning you may fish with this fly.

Work is not a commodity. No one can eat it.
The State has credit.
Property is not capital. Capital is a claim on other men's
services. That is why capital is a ravenous danger.

The evil is not in ownership. The evil is in the claim
on other men's work.   Capital, because of this
claim inherent in it, capital is a ravenous unsleeping
peril. A poison to be watched all the time.

IV

Voices of War

1940–45

1940

Never was the olive
          blossom so thick
                    as that year
for the end of England,
that year for the end
          of Frankreich

10 June
the sound of the bells
          thru the fiddle tone
at 6.30
(about 5.30 p.m.).
Mozart 5th double.

as against the sound of the olive mill
        sound of the stones
             Πόρε Περσεφόνεια
Pore Persephoneia
   who even dead yet hath his mind entire.
against the sound of the olive mill
thud, turn of the stone,
   time of blossom

But here in Tigullio
emerald over sapphire
      april birds thru the stillness
when the fig swells in a fortnight
a far clack of bamboo poles shaking down olives
and the nautile swept in under the cliff, floating reef,
      washed in like lavender blossoms
then stink in the sunlight.

as at Aquila with a hundred heads round the fountain
  where the girls came with their washing, bucato
where the town folk came to get water
    above it an altar to nymphs, to the oreads
where the outlanders offered their gifts
        ὅ οἱ βιότοιο μάλιστα κήδετο οἰκήων
    that had chief care feeding the family
            καλλίροον ὅθεν ὑδρεύοντο πολῖται
with the elms arching over
    'fair flowing' the water
            βωμὸς Νυμφάων

Washed in the Kiang & Han river
      bleached in the autumn sun
皜   what candor
皜   what white horizon –

. . . .

Above this candor, what whiteness
TEXNE, EPISTEME ?
τέχνη ἐπιστήμη
all that we know of things is their sequence
what precedes and what follows   所   所
                          先   先
                          後

PSUKE HYPER TON GASTRON
ψυχὴ ὑπὲρ τὸν γάστρον
cloud like a sea home
  swims under the moon
who with me 且
    the leaf of this plant is shaped like a mouse ear
       仁   when baked figs
       仁   are sold without almonds

To attract the spirits by the beauty of jade
that the music be an announcement to the air between
        earth and heaven
and thrice go up to the roof corner to call the departed spirit
and for a woman that they lay out her party clothes;
        and in her boudoir
            and three times call back her shade

at ten learn by heart the Ta Hsio
& after thirty no bounds to learning
no square or rule to his research
& on the 1ˢᵗ day of that season
the son of heaven   天   sent
                子
his cabinet minister
      goes out to greet the summer
      in the plain south of the capital city

saying: O Kat based upon reason,
    o kat based upon appetite.
First Jove and the earth our mother
  second the sun and moon
    White the pillow of horn, as hard rice grain
    the embroidered shroud glitters as if tattered with fire
    in the end to the same threshold, united

that are the measure of time
Jove and our mother, that are the fountain of all things
Ceres and Liber third
Flora et Regibus
  Flora ac Regibus Robigalia
    lest blight come lest flower come not
Athene, and Cythera, of the olive, of gardens
    to Jove the Vinalia
  to these the wine feasts.
Lympham ac bonum eventum
    without him frustrata est non cultura
and without water all things are dry these are the field gods
O caring dog of Mars
  keep the blight off my grain

Cleopatra or the girl who wrote about currency
Theodora knew all about it
la sposa, imperatore

for which the wind is quiet
        and the sky is clear
freedom not privilege

Fire causeth not beauty,
      nor earth, but the nous
          νοῦς – amor
knowing the handwork,
      closer than fire: more subtle than air
        +
The fire does not make beauty, earth does not make beauty
but the NOUS, the knowing. Closer than fire: more subtle than air
  This effulgence, to spread this effulgence
                  bathed in effulgence

示　明
　　　明

With a white flash of wings over the dawn light
with a flash of wings over sunset
thus cd/ a man learn wisdom
        a man with sky in his heart

in the book of the Odes are 300 poems, and their sole injunction:
                        think straight.

the wise take delight in water
the humane find pleasure in hills
    the knowing put their shoulder to the wheel
            the humane lay hold of the azure.
those who know set their strength to the wheel
            those who know, do.
        intellectus est agens

The holiness of the lord has a blister
& the living temple is full of bugs.
'the light became her grace and dwelt among
blind eyes and shadows' (that are formed as men)
& the rods of the lictor are broken
                        τὸ τῶν Θεῶν πυρός

'The [. . .] is full of observations
                on the monogamy of the indigenes
of Terra del Fuego & the islands off [. . .]'
                Sunday the First of August ex–XXI

So that in August, of the year ex–XXI
        died the czar of Bulgaria
Boris, suddenly, and during that week
and on that day
        stood Massimo, before the door of his pharmacy
with Corrado the oculist; yielding
                'Gazzetta di Genova'
                                1815
which I, quite naturally, borrowed

4. Jan. all goldsmiths, founders, incisors
makers of buttons, embroiderers and all makers, workers,
merchants of whatsoever profession: not to make or sell
any gold object, button, embroidery, bust, emblem, incision
or picture in effigy of Bonaparte or anyone of his family
and this applies to imperial eagles, insignia, and all tokens
of his dominion.
                (Journal des Débats)
        which to the Genovese mind showd zeal; but
scant knowledge of the ways of the human heart

24 Jan. Vienna, that the emperor and his guests
went for a sleigh ride; or procession
on sleighs of gt/ price very ornate . . .
& proud horses, all the nobility,
                Sua Maestà the Emperor, with S.M. the Empress
                                        of the Russias

and S.M. the Emperor of the Russias, with the Princess widow of
Auersperg
His Majesty Denmark with the grandduchess of Weimar
His Majesty Prussia with the countess Zichy-Festetis,
5th the granduke of Baden with
the widow countess Lazansky, and the other sleighs without
order determined; but in every sleigh a prince and a lady.

the sovran sleighs surrounded by pages, and by the noble hungarian
guard
and the grand dukes surrounded by cavalry
with furs of gt splendour   And afterwards drove out
to Schonbrunn, after which returning by torchlight in fine weather
(Gazzetta di Corte)

16 prox. the Czar in Austrian uniform;
this being 'the congress' Maria Louisa;
Schwarzenburg, Wellington /

'leaving Portoferrajo'
his landing . . . before the congress had published
This news reached Genova on March second 'but from
the uncertainty of the rumours'
the Gazzetta did not print it until the eleventh

March 22nd. Later notice from Paris that up till the
fifteenth of this month . . . greatest confidence, and the troops faithful
(to King Bourbon)

Metternich, Talleyrand, Wellington,

P.M. in the Tuileries, says the Moniteur
with the troops that went out this a.m. to impede him
walking in the midst of the populace.

Justice: the Duke of Parma / and has named: Gaeta, Bassano
Molien, the Duke of Otranto.
Page 158/ fondi at 56 and bank stock seven hundred and 67
May 6th in Paris.

May 13th to 16 in Paris
the funds at francs 59 Bank stock at 830
May 20th.   57.50 the funds, bank stock rising to 847
27 and 28/ floating, that is 863, with a set back to 855

First representation, Genova, of the Italian in Algiers, by 'Rosini'

4th June, the funds down to 55, and a fraction and
8 hundred ten for the bank stock.
June 13th   55.25, and the bank at 8 hundred 15.

Genova, July 5th. A Te Deum   to give thanks for the victory.
                        and till July 26th no Paris quotations
          But on July 26, reporting Paris; 16th to 18th.
the funds 62.20, and the bank stock at 990 unruffled.
thereby showing the battle of Vterloo. . .
                  to be that sort of celluloid.

and thereafter/ fluctuant/ never steady/ 2 pts. on the funds;
twenty of the bank stock. up and down/ but
reaching 1030 at the start of October.
          will historians. . . ?

                                        26 Feb. left Elba
                                        Waterloo 15–18 giugno
10 March   81   B. 145
27 March   69.75   980

    after which for an 100 years and for more years
no power stood against usury,
after which, in fact, Mr Malek, the pig faced,
seated on Mrs Taganrog's sofa, said: it will not
take us 20 years to crush Mussolini,
                  and the economic war has begun.
Bonaparte was a goodth manth, it took uth
          twenty yearth to cwuth him, etc.
Napoleon a good man.
          it will not take us etc.
to cwuth Mussolini.
                  35 via Balbo; on Mrs etc's sofa.

name, address, indirizzo, nome, cognome

heroes two a penny & no one kept faith with the dead
& the sunset lemon-green

The cat stars have shut one eye
                over the Sabines
'Sie kann dies als eine Notwendigkeit hinstellen
Sie wird aber niemals eine Entschuldigung finden für die
Tatsache das dies geschen ist ohne den
Verbündeten vorher wenigstens zu verständigen'
            Landeszeitung 30. Cm. 1.Jahrgang nr. 7
            Montag 13 September (1943)

Margherita feeding the pigs with the voice of a
                Fra Angelico angel

Ub. –
  Barnes carte
Nora tea – uova
aerop. 2 soldat
group peasants. 'a Rieti'
7 Bagni   vino pane   vino pesante   vin. generosum
Fara Sabina   carab.
  aerop. & campo

                                        'siamo solo donne'

ucelli   grido gatti
break[fast]   jam
  carozza   shop 4 pesche
uova – uva   Rieti. acqua
    osteria. vino amaro.
        dormito.
        camions   no
auto borghese idiota 2 k[m].
    vino cativo
cena – contadini – minestra doppia

Maderno, and there was calm in the stillness/
Mt. Fugi rose of Garda, and the cat walked on the narrow rail.
In September the barbaciani cried catlike from
tree to tree in the Alban stillness/
                                    In November on Gardasee
There was stillness:
            The quiet outlasting all wars.
This said Eumolpas is a German, who says that he is American.
Will you stay for the night,
of   the twin cat's eyes   one was shut over
        the via Salaria; and time was not.
And Rome was down, down,
                        'we have no officers
what ought we to do?'

Where did you get that book, said the attaché.
'To the same threshold' in the end to the same threshold,
the ivory neck-rest is hard as new rice grains;
and the silk-shroud gleams as if tattered with fire.

    'who will be here at sunrise'.

Fugi rose of Benacus,
    not yet capo provincial   Gioacchino

Now that the world's walls are falling,
                and world's word must stand alone

voice harder than marble
only by greatest precision / can any force attain to
 power of changing
when the axe handle is hewing, the model is not
far distant/ thus men are used to rule men.

the archer who misses the bullseye, seeks the why in himself.

when the gov't was straight,

 like an arrow

when the gov't was bad,

 ... like an arrow

360 thousand and sorrow, sorrow like rain
said a refugee from Fiume
'Ciao, Fausto' and you wd/ have seen tears falling 'come una pioggia'
Then beaten like nautilus on the rock
But in the train thus by Padova
      going back to Fiume.
 old mother weeping, her son
Anzac, Gallipoli
     sorrow, sorrow like rain
to their boats at Piraeus, under Stukas
   30 thousand or 50 thousand
      hurled against cliffs under Athens
Hakenkreuz on Olympus
   Thermopoli, Marathon
'passed thru the town of Thebes in pursuit of the enemy' . . .
approximately 50 thousand gross registered tons . . .

rise mass, rise bulk, in the lee shore under the cliff
   sat the Possum curling his tail in the moonlight
    and singing as no man ever
ὁδὸς ἀθάνατος
     ἀθάνατ᾽ ἀοιδή

So that he put up a saw mill, and they took him
to fight over in Africa;
and after that war was over he started a small commercio
and they took him to fight in Greece and Albania:
  and they were five thousand in a cup of the hills
                              wholly surrounded;
    and for six months with frozen feet
      and provisions by a rope over the cliff
or from one Albanian, with whom they exchanged rice for
provisions:
and 'there were doctors in the front line' were there?
there was four miles of mule track for the wounded:
and when the stretcher bearers got to the front line
                      they gave 'em rifles:
            who had never touched a rifle before:
and the rest propaganda; and no letters arrived from home
but an airplane brought after months a paper;
that told of the bombardment of Genova;
        the house where he lived and his children
and no news for three months after that
and to get his family allowance, when suspended;
he finally got it by tipping the doorman
'these things wear you down professore'

where the earth stank of blood & will for five autumns
insomma l'umanità non è canaglia
                          Filippo di Stefano
        ants come to house seeking water

m'apparve in quel triedro:
                    'Io son la luna'
driven from my house on the cliff side.
And by this mulatiera Sigismundo
coming to Genova, to set his hand to a treaty, as witness
Lorenzo the shade of a shade, but above me Confucio
held in the air a space,
                              for a space Gautama,
How is it? I said: that the ghosts are so gathered?
and from the high bank over the wave, came an answer:
nel gran periplo, the sun gathers his fleet to our shore
thus are they with you, thus hang in the aether
thus walk in yr/ hill paths

Here Scotus; who said: all are lights
Scotus Erigena   Quae sunt, omnia lumina

And I: 'Sordello's words are still with us,
mi pare Cunizza'; 'Aye, Cunizza'.

The sun in his great periplum . . . .
                    gathers his fleet to our shore
I am involved . . . For whom the bell tolls.

            WAN / his splendour consisted
            in knowing where to stop.
            Magnificent his coherence

sure he's over there on the other soide wid dh christians
but he will be runing off down into the owld pagody
      every now an then
to take a swat at the Florentines: and being at bottom eyetalyan
he looks wid a bad eye suspicious on whatever comes from
outside of there, or at any rate he cant take a rale intherest

sure but the owld hook nose meant well; he had a koind heart in
  him after all   when he cd/ foind it.
. . .
Bigob oi tink oi putt him on dh roight track wid that translation
of Dionysius/   He had koindly intentions
as in that letter to the big BowWow Can Grande
thought it was useful to the commonweal/   no bleatin aesthete
      qt/ epist/ C.G.

               Ant. Pius/ not from others' misfortune
               Cheu: bros/ same bks/
               Brancus/ mais nous
                     7 to = Kung.
           sure something dat wont sqush when he sits on it
something like a mathematical series/ like two and two equal four
that wont squash when he leans up ferninst it.
      and dere are udder tings loick that, say Confucius;
fer instance/ things solid
You dont know what dey are/ oi dont know what dey are

            but something He can sit down on
all things dat are are loights
                              Dante/ sense/ not the thing but the time

V

Italian Drafts

1944–1945

Accade ogni mezzo secolo una meraviglia.
Entrai l'Albergo Pace e c'era una bottiglia
                    Bologna gran spumante
e ricordai tutto:
ricordai Rimbaud all'Albergo Verde
e ricordai Iseult, ch'era il grande amore.

Che una guerra sopra un'altra,
                        non è meraviglia,
che si muore, non si muore
                    dura tutto
                        nell'akasa, tutto dura.
Che una guerra segue un'altra, nulla conta,
nell'akasa. Mi ricordai
che nel mezzo la tragedia
Sergent e l'altro parlavano della pesca d'aragosta
    'not a counter among the lot'
            a Terranova
                    ma 'na guerra . . .

Sotto la Rupe Tarpeia: 'che i dei romani' torneranno
    ed essi capivano, era nell'anno nove forse
ma i DEI R0MANI . . .
    hanno distrutto le cave, sfrattato il gerente
                            grotte vuote
Ma i DEI R0MANI son tornati
ed a Teracina

Every half century a marvel occurs.
I entered the Albergo Pace and there was a big bottle
                  Bologna gran spumante
and I remembered it all:
I remembered Rimbaud at the Cabaret-Vert
and I remembered Iseult, who was the great love.

That one war comes upon another
                        is no wonder
That one dies, or doesn't die
                        everything lasts
                        in the akasa, everything.
That one war follows another, nothing matters,
in the akasa. I remembered
      that in the middle of tragedy
Sargent and the other one talked of lobster fishery
      'not a counter among the lot'
            in Newfoundland
                  but one war . . .

Under the Rupe Tarpeia: 'that the Roman gods' shall return
      and they understood, it was the ninth year perhaps
but the ROMAN GODS . . .
      they have destroyed the quarries, evicted the headman.
                              empty grottoes
But the ROMAN GODS have returned
and at Terracina

        son tornati
                con gli occhi chiusi onniveggenti
e la forma citerea, dove non fu che piedestallo
  ma ora: C'è la DEA
  che sta sul piedestallo e guarda il cielo e'l mare
non è sepolta
    madre d'Eros
        e non muore ella,
                ed io ricordo
ch'era scesa le scale un po' incerta
                        un po' distratta
  ed eterna dura
        Κόρη καὶ δήλια

                    returned
                        with closed eyes   all-seeing
and the Cytheraean form, where there was only the pedestal
    but now: There's the GODDESS
    who stands on the pedestal and gazes on sky and sea
she is not buried
                    mother of Eros
                        and she does not die,
                                and I remember
how she came down the stairs a little uncertain
                            a little absent-minded
            and lasts eternally
                    Κόρη καὶ δήλια

Ripresero allora i dolci suoni
ch'accompagnarono la frase interrotta
          di Galla dell'Esarcato
                    i cui cavalieri la tenevan bordone
il cigolar, e'l contrapunto
nel zaffiro mite del aere di quel orizzonte
prima che Febo fu ai merli giunto

Poi dove la salita pare scendere per un triedro
          fra rocce grigie nel oliveto
               sotto l'imagine e fano di Maria
incontrai una compagnia di persone
          che parevan di carnevale a prima vista
               'Doutz brais e critz' cantaron in compagnia
finché io riconobbine una e fui mosso a dire . . .

Then again the sweet sounds began
which accompanied the interrupted phrase
        of Galla of the Exarchate,
            whose knights provided the burden
the twittering, and the counterpoint
in the mild sapphire of that horizon's atmosphere
before Phoebus had reached the battlements

Then, where the path seems to descend through a triedro
    among the grey rocks in the olive grove
    under the image of Mary's chapel
I met a peopled company
    who at first sight seemed a carnival
            'Doutz brais e critz' they sang in company
until I recognized one woman and was moved to say . . .

In un triedro dell'oliveto m'apparve
ed ella: Tiranno lo chiamano,
   ma non tradiva i suoi, mio gran fratello.

Cunizza, le tue be'e chiome, color di rame e d'oro,
ancor vaghezzon
                    chi sa di verso e rima.

Quello che feci, or è disfatto in parte
            non domandar di me, ma dà nuova arte
                    non torno più, né devo più fatica
            a rivestir ombra, dico ombra ch'ombra proietta
            non cerchi di me aiuto perch'io non torno
                        cercate novella arte, cercate un Duccio
                    o un nuovo Pisanello;
non entro più la porta
                del bordello umano
                    né metto piede in terra, crepa chi crepa
Domandan se in paradiso entra disprezzo
                    in cima a questo monte
dico di SÌ, come già detto fu
                    in pietra e 'n marmo
                ed ha già durato, e tu hai il sigillo
Tanto del vero lasciai colà scolpito
            nulla di me avrai oltre quello
di chi rima
                    negus vezer mon bel pensar no val

In a triedro of the olive grove she appeared to me
and she: 'Tyrant they call him,
    but he, my great brother, never betrayed his own'.

'Cunizza, your beautiful tresses, colour of copper and gold
still entice
                those who are skilled in verse and rhyme.'

'What I did is now partly undone
    don't ask for me, but for new art
            I won't return, nor must labour again
        to put on a shadow, I mean a shadow that casts a shadow
        don't expect help from me because I won't return
            look for new art, look for a Duccio
            or a new Pisanello;
I will not pass again the door
    of the human brothel
        nor will I tread the ground, let die who will,
They ask if in paradise there is contempt
        on the summit of this mountain
I answer YES, as has already been said
            in stone and marble
        and has already lasted – and you have the seal
so much of the truth I left there sculpted
    and beyond this you'll have nothing of me
those who rhyme
            negus vezer mon bel pensar no val

cui legge i versi, e sa ancor cantarli
        avrà di me ricordo.

'Donna', dissi io, 'cogli occhi di falco,
sentir parlar di te e de la Pia
ancor nel cuor gentil desta disio.
più che l'amor risplende qui l'ardire.
Qui son Flaminio ed Augurello,
    versi di non falsa zecca.
Chi sa leggere i versi di Sordello . . .
Negus vezer mon bel pensar no val,
si canta ancora. Dillo al tuo drudo
che il suo canto dura,
    e'l suon d'onda al battito.

Ma chi è questo che pare di linea fatto
e senza lume e trasparente,
che vedo gli ulivi dietro?'

'Ombra sono e ombra fui'
mi venne dal diafano formato
'quando io scrissi l'Isoteus,
ma ombra che seppe il greco.
Tu sei, perché amasti.
Ma vivo quel giorno nella lizza
    perché amai Omero
    misurando i miei versi contro i suoi
    plasmando i miei sul suo modello.
Passò di qui il Sigismondo?'

Ed io: 'A Zena? A Genova,
per Via Aurelia Antica, distratto.
Scendeva da San Pantaleone, per la vecchia via
            lungo Pan t'Helion
come andando a Genova, per firmare'.

Né più la vidi, ma anzi una favilla
color di Marte scese
calda come sull'incudine il ferro martellato, e rovente.

who read the lines, and still know how to sing them
            will have memory of me.'

'Woman with hawk-eyes', I said,
'to hear talk of you and of la Pia
still awakens the gentle heart's desire
here courage more than love shines forth.
Here be Flaminius and Augurellus,
    verses not falsely minted.
Who can read Sordello's verses . . .
Negus vezer mon bel pensar no val,
is still sung. Tell your paramour
that his song endures,
        and the wave sound to the beat.

But who is this who seems made up of lines
and without light and transparent,
so that I see the olive trees behind him?'

'I am a shadow and was a shadow'
came to me from the formed diafan
'when I wrote the Isoteus,
but a shadow who knew Greek.
You are because you loved.
But I live that day in the tournament
    because I loved Homer
    measuring my verses against his
    shaping mine according to his model.
Has Sigismund passed here?'

And I: 'To Zena? To Genoa,
along Via Aurelia Antica, absent-minded.
He was going down from San Pantaleone, along the old road
            along Pan t'Helion
as if on his way to Genoa, to sign'.

Nor did I see him longer, but rather a spark
colour of Mars descended
hot as iron hammered on the anvil, and scalding.

Era in divisa
    non d'infermiera con la croce rossa
anzi in braghe e camicia
che andava a rastrellare
Donna cogli occhi di falco

'Imola', mi rispose,
ed io vidi le mura, e sentii la risposta
'Sforza fui, come tu indovini, indomata,   *Riario*
costa che costa, tu hai la mia risposta.
Ne ho ancora lo stampo, che alzò la gonna
a Forlì contro ogni minaccia
dalle mura nel fumo della battaglia
questo accadde nel Quattrocentonovantotto.
                Da un pezzo dubito della mia semenza
poi da luglio in luglio, subbuglio
stercofagi   male di famiglia
                    andar in basso col correr degli anni
                    può arrivar lunge
            pare almeno che mai si rialza, o sarà rialzato'.
                    Né parlò più con me, né io con ella
    res nec verba
    wheat from weed
ma gli occhi io rividi d'una che porta divisa
e vidi le mura e la cittadella
e sentii come sferzata:
'Perché non porti le armi?'

Ed ella poi salì,
né vidi più che il baco, color di raggio
di divina seta, tela del sole, profeta:

'In su son troni.
In su regge il loto dove son Budda e Confucio.
Gautama Budda nel suo sogno eterno,
    che dà l'eterna legge
        a chi in terra vive già beato.
Troni son due:
sogna bellezza eterna l'indiano,

She wore a uniform
   not a Red Cross nurse's
      rather trousers and shirt
      on her way to round up suspects
Hawk-eyed woman

   'Imola', she answered
and I saw the walls and heard the answer
'Sforza I was, as you guess, untamed,   *Riario*
cost what it may, you have my response.
I still have the mould, who lifted her skirt
at Forlì defying all threats
from the walls in the smoke of battle
this happened in fourteen-ninety-eight.
For some time I have doubted my seed
then from July to July, hurly-burly
eaters of excrement   family-illness
         to go down with the run of the years
         can be long
at least it appears that it never recovers, or will be recovered'.
         Nor spoke further to me; nor I to her.
   res nec verba
   wheat from weed
but I saw again the eyes of one who wears a uniform
and saw the walls of the citadel
and felt like a whip-lash:
'Why don't you bear arms?'

And then she rose,
and I perceived but a cocoon, colour of ray
of divine silk, sun's web, prophetic:

'Above are thrones.
Above rises the lotus where are Buddha and Confucius
Gautama Buddha in his eternal dream,
   who gives the eternal law
      to those who on earth already live in blessedness.
Two thrones there are:
the Indian dreams of beauty eternal

il bell'agir è parte di Confucio
a chi costruisce o regge impero
o fonda dinastia duratura
e dà la misura
sopra quell'acqua che mai non s'impura,
                    eterna fonte.

Giù, giù per l'Ida corrono le ragazze
gentili spiriti di Grecia antica.
    Demofonte,
che mai d'amor *traiz pena*,
                        ha conforto.
Douz brais e critz
    qui cantan trovatori
fra gli uzelli di foresta eterna.

Yrmindrudis, perfecta Palladis arte,
auro subtilis serica fila parans,
pepla mariti
            col filo d'oro
                        ricamò.

good action is Confucius's part
for the individual who constructs or governs an empire
or establishes a lasting dynasty
and gives the measure
over the water that never stales,
    eternal fount.'

Down, down from Ida run the girls
the gentle spirits of ancient Greece
   Demophon,
who never of love *traiz pena*
                 has comfort.
Douz brais e critz
             here troubadours sing
among the birds of the eternal wood.

Yrmindrudis   perfecta Palladis arte
auro subtilis serica fila parans,
pepla mariti
       with gold thread
           embroidered

Il Sol gran ammiraglio conduce la sua flotta
   nel suo gran periplo,
conduce la flotta sotto i nostri scoglie.
   Anchise sentì così cantar le donnine
che lamentarono Primavera Morta, che tu che accosta
questi nostri prati, senti le voci delle ninfe liete
a radere la nostra bella pianura ora le barche delle pianete,
     non cercate fra loro i vostri,
lo sangue li apporta a migliaia
    che cadon fra nebbia e neve, a migliaia
    e i fiocchi giaccion e fondon. . .
Fondon e giaccion i fiocchi sotto l'Aprile
  questo Eurota porta
     ch'Euro scorta
      ovvero Volturno
come i latini dicono qualche volta.

        Là nel borgo altro, coi cristiani
     indugia un po' sul suo grattacielo
   per chiacchierar, e per sfogar rancori
  va anche lì a cerca d'argomento, e di sentir novelle
da Firenze, al piano dell'orgoglio

a radere nostri liti, la pianura
  piena di prati e di tanti fiori

14 Jan

The Sun great admiral conducts his fleet
    in his great periplum
conducts his fleet under our cliffs
    thus Anchises heard the girls sing
who mourned Dead Spring, so that you who approach
our lawns, you hear the voices of the happy nymphs
now the boats of the planets shave our beautiful plain,
    do not seek among them your own,
the blood carries them here by the thousands
    who fall in fog and snow, by the thousands
    and the flakes fall and melt
melt and fall the flakes under April
    this Eurota brings
      whom Eurus follows
      or Volturnus
      as the Latins say sometimes.

        There in the other burg, with the Christians
      he lingers a little on his skyscraper,
    to chat, and air grievances
  he goes there also to look for a subject, to hear the news
of Florence, at the plain of pride

to shave our shores, the plain
  full of lawns and of many flowers

di canti lieti, e regionar d'amore

Sest Empirico
(Calvo e Gallo, Licoris)

Quintilia io mi chiamai, quest'è Licore.

frutto maledetto dell'eterno puzzo
    perversione d'ogni buon istinto
    nel pozzo nero ogni luce muore
    indegna dell'alto dono, e razza morta

quel ch'io costrussi fu del mio stipendio e braccio   Sig/
    Mise la crusca nel pane di Cristo
                        troppo misto
merce sul mercato
    compra al dieci e vende poi al cento

Né più son vita e fiamma
            (gran ombra con poca fiamma)   *Savonarola*
    pel bene ch'io feci ho questo perduto.
        d'intenzione io non fui maligno
non del tutto fiammo
            condusse mia città alla rovina
pur combinando pace (Napoli)
                    e quando potei evitando violenza
                    altrui errore
strinse: e minacciando fame
come hanno ora appreso i grossi giudei
                    goder dell'indugio
bel frutto fu, ma di sì mala pianta
ed alla lunga rovinò il giardino:
far del male per averne bene
            eredità di bello e di brutto.

Savonarola furibondo nell'altro eccesso
distrusse i liuti, arte di lana, per male dell'usura
        Fiandra: raso, serge, rozzo
perdendo il produrre delle fabbriche dei telai
            i telai di saja e rascia
ci fa profitto e perde il telaio

of happy songs, and talk of love
                    Sextus Empiricus
                    (Calvus and Gallus, Licoris)
    Quintilia I was called, this is Licoris

accursed fruit of the eternal stink
  perversion of every good instinct
  in the black sewer all light dies
  unworthy of the high gift, and race defunct

what I have built was with my stipend and arm   *Sigismund*
  He put bran in the bread of Christ
                    too mixed
wares on the market
    buys at ten and sells for one hundred

Nor yet am I life and flame
        (great shadow with small flame)   *Savonarola*
    for the good I did, I lost this
        in intention I was not malevolent
I do not wholly burn
                    he brought my city to ruin
though arranging peace (Naples)
            and avoiding violence when I could
                others' error
he tightened: and threatening hunger
what now big Jews have learned
                to profit from delay
a fine fruit he was, but of so ill a tree
and in the end he laid the garden waste:
to do evil seeking good
                inheritance of beauty and ugliness

Savonarola furious in his high excess
 destroyed the lutes, art of wool, through evil of usury
    Flanders: satin, serge, rough
losing the product of the mills of looms
                the looms of saja and rascia
he makes profit and loses the loom

per pronto lucro perde il telaio
    albero pel zolfo
se vuol entrare, cercate prima la porta
a creare non si arriva coll'acquisto
        fiamma mista

fra mala erba sta questo po' di vero
      farne dove non era, gran mistero
        distrussero i simboli del bel pensiero

                Cos/ to Nic. d'Est
                cambio della moneta

Lo bons reis Carolus: nella cui corte
    Erigena teneva bel discorso   *Yrmintruda*
        filava e bordava la Regina   *druda*
serviva il marito, e li fece camicia.
        Dottor Ilare, rispettò la ragione:
        bontà di Dio ebbe in guiderdone
d'ogni cielo è fatto cittadino.
        filava a filo d'oro
        al fuso ed al pennecchio

Giù nel giardino formale
            di marmo e cipressi
ma nell'ombra
        leggera malinconia
con gran danno di piccola favella
                (tregenda)
Lorenzo: 'Nerone ebbe ragione   *Diotisalvi*
        bella persona nasconde spirocheta
           avvelenò la stirpe
      difficile viver ricco senza aver lo stato.
Poco dura. Ombra io sono, non sono vita e fiamma,
    mi sento monco d'eterna fiamma'.

Ed io: 'Vostri bei versi caro e gran Lorenzo
si cantano qua giù, a la memoria'

for quick gain loses the loom
        tree for sulphur
you who want to enter, find the door first
creation is not attained by acquisition
            mixed flame

  among rank weeds there is this little truth
        make a great mystery where there was none
        destroyed the symbols of fine thought

                Cosimo to Nicolò d'Este
                exchange of coin

Lo bons reis Carolus, in whose court
  Erigena held fine discourse
        the queen wove and embroidered   *Ermentrude*
she served her husband, and made him a shirt   *paramour*
        Doctor Hilaritas respected reason
        God's bounty he received in compensation
of all heavens he has been given the freedom
        Wove with gold thread
        at the spindle and the flax

Down in the formal garden
        of marble and cypress
but in the shadow
        a slight melancholy
with great damage from little speech
                (pandemonium)
Lorenzo: 'Nerone was right   *Diotisalvi*
  beauteous person hides spirochete
        he poisoned the race
  it is difficult to live rich without owning the state
Lasts little. Shadow I am, am not life and flame
        I feel void of eternal flame'.

And I: 'Your lovely verses, dear and great Lorenzo
are sung down here, in memory'

'e molto e distinzion, conservo forma
e questo parco è pieno di bellezza:
rimango traccia nella mente altrui
            né piccolo destino, né io rimpiango troppo
dilettante
            e per quello mi è concesso in balia'.

mi pareva di prender quota e i miei occhi vedevano
in riposo Gautama sul loto, e Confucio stesso
colla faccia al Meridiano, e nel mezzo all'aria
    chi sembrava Kuan Yin, col ramoscello
    poi la nebbia si richiudeva dorata

'and much and distinction, I keep form
and this park is full of beauty:
I remain trace in the mind of others
    not a small destiny, nor do I much regret
dilettante
        and for this it is given me to command'

I seemed to be soaring and my eyes beheld
in repose Gautama on the lotus, and Confucius himself
his face to the Meridian, and in middle air
    one who looked like Kuan Yin, with the branch
    then again the golden mist closed up

Dove la salita scende e fa triedro
   mi veniva scalza incontro
e notai che no portava né cestino né fazzoletto pieno
   non mi sembrò nota, neppure ignota,
ed io: non siete del nostro clivo
   non porti uova o altro pel mercato
e nondimeno . . .
                        ed ella: Il tetto è rotto
Delle Grazie è caduto in mar
                              per i bombardieri
   vado da Pantaleo per riposarmi
                           E sei? dissi io
e sparì
         ed io voltai
              e non era di già mi dietro

come legno, e non soffrì dal freddo della notte
   pur se Dicembre fu
                    e 'l mare di bronzo
nel mar un disco enorme di bronzo dove batteva il sole
   il resto era piatto e piombo.

Where the path descends and makes a triedro
   she came towards me barefoot
and I noticed that she carried no basket nor full handkerchief
   she appeared neither known nor unknown
and I: You are not from our hillside
   you carry no eggs nor anything to market
      and nonetheless . . .
              she answered: The roof is broken
Delle Grazie has been cast into the sea
                    by the bombers
   I am on my way to Pantaleo to rest
         And your name? I asked
and she vanished
   and I turned
      and she was no longer behind me

like wood, and did not suffer of the night's cold
   though this was December
         and the sea of bronze
in the sea an enormous bronze disk where the sun beat
   the rest was flat and lead.

Mai con codardi (codini) sarà l'arte monda
lascia che i Dei ritornano fra di voi. . .
        e con questo
Ave Maris Stella mi suonò all'orecchio, per l'aria serale
e col ramo io la vidi
come Kuanina, col ramo di salce
                    vidi l'eterna dolcezza
formata: di misericordia la madre, dei mari protettrice,
    soccorso in naufragio, manifesto
sempre rivista a Prato, e a Monte Rosa
    'il Fano delle Grazie è in rovina' mi disse
                    a Pantaleo mi rifugio, la sfollata
    dalla Dorata, sempre cacciata
vaga, invicta; Lucina dolentibus, sono così lunare
    di bachi protettrice; umile; duratura,
Il pargoletto mi ama, ch'io nutro
                            Io son la Luna
non son la Sofia; anzi la temo
    ieratica, mosaicata
Sofia Hecate, nemmeno conosco,
                    mai incoronata nell'alta sfera
ieratica, stato lontano: danneggia, taglia, terrore.

Io son la cacciata. Io, da Giove amata: mesta,
errante. Europa mi chiamai, sotto le stelle dell'Orsa
    sotto gli ulivi, vista da te olim
mio marito zappava sul clivo

Never with cowards (fogies) will art be mended
let the Gods return among you
  and with this
Ave Maris Stella sounded in my ear, in the evening air
and with the branch I saw her
as Kuanon, with the willow branch,
        saw the eternal sweetness
 formed: of compassion the mother, of seas protector
  aid in shipwreck, manifest
yet seen again at Prato, and at Monte Rosa
   the shrine delle Grazie is ruined, she said to me
        to Pantaleo I repair, homeless
     from the Dorata, forever driven out
vaga, invicta; Lucina dolentibus, so lunar am I
  protectress of cocoons; humble, enduring
The little boy loves me, whom I nurse
                I am la Luna
I am not Sophia, in fact I fear her
     hieratic, mosaic'd
Sophia Hecate also I do not know
            never crowned in the high sphere
hieratic, remote state – harms, severs: terror.

I am the driven out. Io, beloved of Jove: sad,
wandering. Europa I was called under the stars of the Bear
  under the olives, olim seen by you
my husband hoed the hill

il mio sposo novello
col pargoletto sedevo, tu m'hai visto
non son Sofia, anzi la temo
i codini non son miei amici
    io son la cacciata
nemmeno Artemide m'è amica: il pargoletto mi ama
che io nutro, io son la Luna, e il latte,
troppo spiegar ti sarà presuntuoso,
                Pietà mi chiamai anche
mio figlio è morto: Io son l'assunta.

                Salmasio
che fu tiranno, non falso ai suoi

mare che s'imbronza; bello in dicembre
dove il sol si fa martello
                o specchio abbagliante

my new bridegroom
with the little boy I sat, you saw me
I am not Sophia, in fact I fear her
fogies are not my friends
    I am the driven out
nor yet Artemis is my friend: the little boy loves me
whom I feed, I am la Luna, and the milk,
too much explaining would be presumptuous to you
                Pietà I was also called
my son is dead: I am the Assunta

                Salmasius
who was a tyrant, not false to his own

sea that turns to bronze; beautiful in December
where the sun becomes a hammer
                    or blinding mirror

Ogni beato porta con sé il cielo,
   di qui dipende,
di qui proviene la letizia sua, e la sua forza
         in sé congiunto, nel suo dovunque,
Il raggio di Citera si fa stella in quel punto
      dove converge
sun servant of nature.
      Cunizza forma chiara! poi involta, né vidi che il baco
         adagio saliva: come una nube
      che va a spasso, senza fretta, né premura
nel calmo azzurro

più bella è, più grande è il pericolo

serpente, neschek: guastò il paradiso
cotal gran danno da piccola favella
      quel po' di vero nei maledetti pianti,
fatto mistero dove non è mistero
      fatto gran buio, dove non fu mistero
         apposta fatto: per spargere distruzione
            largire, propagar veleno
                  tregenda

armonia distingue, divide nota da nota
      non perdendo la qualità, né proprio essere
non rassomigliando, anzi
         Erigena on Dante

Every blessed soul carries along with it the heavenly sphere
    from which it depends,
this is the source of its delight, and force
    joined in itself, in its everywhere
The ray of Cythera becomes a star at that point
                                where it converges
        sun servant of nature.
'Cunizza clear form!' – then swathed, saw but the cocoon
            slowly rising: as a cloud
    that walks about, without haste, nor hurry
in the quiet blue

the more beautiful she is, the greater the peril

serpent, neschek; wasted paradise
such great damage from small speech
        the little truth in the damned laments,
    mystery created where there is no mystery
        great darkness created, where was no mystery
        done on purpose; to spread destruction
                to produce, propagate poison
                    pandemonium

harmony distinguishes, divides note from note
    not losing quality, nor own being
not resembling, on the contrary
                Erigena on Dante

Lorenzo, St. Amb/
ho questo perdono

Lor/ contro violenza, scaltrezza
        sfruttai, né giova al commercio l'usura,
    lucro adesso: perdendo i telai, privilegio d'indugio
Sig/ non dall'usura, né cambio di moneta

Lorenzo, St Ambrose
I have this pardon

Lorenzo against violence, shrewdness
  I exploited, nor does usury help business,
   present profit: losing the looms, privilege of delay
Sigismund not by usury, nor exchange of money

Nel periplo che fa il vostro Sole
ammiraglio delle pianete, servo di natura
    rade le nostre scoglie
colla sua flotta, la barca sua rade la nostra piana
e le scoglie di borde, la sua barca ci accosta
or stando in mare, ed ora di vicino

    accosta i ripi e scoglie della pianura nostra,
della pianura sì bella, dove cantiamo a spasso
con tutta la sua flotta, or Gea, sua, vostra
or la stella Marte

        lo sangue chiama a noi
    quando è sparso, come ora è sparso

da me non hai bisogno che io ti spiego
non cerco i vostri: a migliaia cadon e giaccion
    sotto fra neve e nebbia

In the periplum that your Sun makes
admiral of the planets, servant of nature
                              shaves our cliffs
with his fleet, his boat shaves our plain
and the cliffs' edge, his boat accosts us
now staying in the sea, now closer

   accosts the shores and cliffs of our plain,
of the plain so beauteous, where we sing as we walk about
with his entire fleet, now Gea, his, yours
now the star of Mars

      blood calls to us
when it is spilled; as now it is spilled

from me you do not need an explanation
I do not seek your people
          by thousands they fall and lie
                          in snow and fog

e i fiocchi giaccion e fondon
                    sotto l'Aprile
quando Volturno porta
          (vento che i greci chiamano Euro)
i canti lieti e ragionar d'amore
Qui Hylas, qui sono Ione e Flora ed Alcmene
          Dione, Hylas e Clymene
          più più profondo ancora, Dirce
        pur del passato vostro son le ombre
                              ma non le nuove
e chi scrisse Felicity Taverner
e quella di Lencour verrà ed Astrea
                    e Verdenal aspetta il suo amico

né seppi il tempo
          né se il passato fu né se 'l domani
ma gran pace ebbi nel cuor, in dormiveglia così sereno
          dove la mente veglia
                    né l'intelletto agogna
          né corpo sente il freddo
                    Aliscans senza urto

e come eco lontana:
        Sappiamo i vostri fatti, o gran Ulixe
    e quel che a Troia facesti
così l'attimo del gran respiro
          porta il sereno fra le vostre stragi.

and the snowflakes lie and melt
                        under April
when Volturnus
            (whom Greeks call Eurus)
carries the happy songs and reasoning of love
Here Hylas, here Ione and Flora and Alcmena
                Dione, Hylas and Clymene
                and deeper down, Dirce
            these are also the shadows of your past
                            but not the new ones
and she who wrote Felicity Taverner
and Vail of Lencour shall come and Astraea
                and Verdenal awaits his friend

nor did I know the time
                nor if this was the past or the morrow
but I had great peace in my heart, in such a serene drowsiness
                where the mind is alert
                        nor the intellect desires
                nor body feels cold
                        Aliscamps without pressure

and as a distant echo:
            We know your feats, O great Ulysses
        and what you have done at Troy
thus the moment of a great breathing
                brings serenity among your slaughters

Come è ch'io sento le vetuste voci
più che mai prima chiare e più sovente
pur se 'l disio era prima in non minor misura?

                              il processo
muove ad agio ed in stagione
come la luce che è veloce, non affrettata
ogni cosa alla velocità sua: senza fretta
prende la lezione che vede nella natura del processo

alla stagione torni, quando il giro sia compiuto
ora, non ora   non stagna   non è fissa: anzi muove
secondo la sua natura   ogni anima felice   può tornarci,
     un stagione 'nella sua felicità'
          sì che a Metastasio pensai; e quasi lo vidi.
                         niente subbuglio

          così l'armonia distingue,   e la nota
     divide da nota, sempiterna
                              nulla è mutata:
nulla se perde; né cambia l'essere suo duraturo
e nulla stagna, perché in vita è moto
          eterno *ens* causa di moto
                         causa ed asse che non vacilla
fuor di quel ente che non mai vacilla

nulla   ogni velocità e nota d'armonia

How is it that I hear the ancient voices
clearer and more frequently than ever before
though formerly desire was no weaker?

                        the process
moves at ease and in season
as light that is speedy, not hurried
every thing at its own speed: without hurry
it learns the lesson it sees in the nature of the process

to the season you return, when the cycle is completed
now, not now   doesn't stagnate   isn't fixed: rather moves
according to its nature   every happy soul   can return there,
   in season 'in its own happiness'
       so that I thought of Metastasio; and nearly saw him.
                   no confusion

      thus distinguishes harmony,   and note
divides from note, sempiternal
               nothing is changed:
nothing is lost; nor does its durable being change
and nothing stagnates, because life is motion
      eternal *ens* cause of motion
             cause and axis that does not wobble
besides that essence that never wobbles

nothing   every speed and note of harmony

perché la porta che è aperta a tutti
    sì pochi scelgon per entrarvi dentro

che perde pazienza, il ben che perde, col lume d'intelletto

suonatore
    che non di tasto, ma di tempo sbaglia

why the door that is open to all
        so very few choose to enter

who loses patience, the good he loses, with the light of the intellect

a musician
        missing not the key but the tempo

Se in febbraio il freddo rilascia la morsa
e quel santo che ama l'amore chiam'all'amore
e suona CRAS AMET da ogni siepe
e da ogni oliveto 't'amet, amet' risponde
in contrapunto
                              e il giovinozz' va in baldanza
              e il vecchio si ringiova
così io mi sciolsi a sentir la loro canzone
e il bel tepore dell'aer sembrava dorata
              ma senza sole ch'io vidi

If in February frost relaxes its bite
and the saint who loves loving summons everyone to love
and CRAS AMET resounds from every hedge
and from every olive grove 't'amet, amet' answers
in counterpoint
                    and the youth becomes bold
                              and the old man rejuvenates
I melted in listening to their song
and the fine mild air seemed golden
          but without any sun that I could see

VI

Pisa

1945

a quando?
   the grass round the tent pole moves nel vento Tireno
aspetto la diana –
Past Malmaison in field by the river the tables of the pavillion
Sirdar – Pre Catelan, Armenonville –
on the island the author of the
Cat & the Cherub emerged from
a past 12 years distant
at Ventadour the keys of the chateau
had been left before 1790 @ the cottage
where you may still find them
& the rain @ Ussel beat all the night in blind fury
Nancy out of the 90' at Perigueux,
                  e ad Arli
in that room Napoleon the bis
in this other room no man
                  ΟΥ ΤΙΣ

so his eminence, the eminent Possum
      visited the Dordogne cavernes –
& our eminent confrere mistrusted
      the authorship & antiquity
of the designs on post cards – but if not Picasso –
who faked 'em.

                  & old Ionides
had taken extreme dislike to

Napoleon barbiche
near him @ a reception – remembering
Swinburne & Howell the pirate

Violet's garden Natalie's garden
   with the old trees propped up.
Harriet's lawn once seen –
     as subaqueus –
the tower at Leacock   ΟΥ ΤΙΣ
  'A L'Amitié'
      (Voltaire Louis XIV)
à Mme du Chatelet. La LeCouvreur
cherry & apple wood or
    scent of the fig branch burning.
'I have always' sd. old Blunt
from his four-poster, 'always gone on
   the principle – when in doubt –
do it' –
   a long life & a, on the whole,
                    happy one –

'a german' sd. the man out of Naxos
    (epic), 'who says he
is an american'. will you stay for the night.
& the peasants wd not take pay for the minestra
nor the old woman for her fresh egg
nor at Settebagni for bread,
   after the vino was pd. for.
water they brought from the spring
This up after Fara Sabina over the buried ruins
the barbagianni cried in the night
         to barbagianni
and catcall, & the redbearded lawyer
     complained of the zizzania
     spread by dispersing tramps –
  thus going out of modernity
    past Fara Sabina. –
'we have no officers, what ought we to do?'
   sd. the boys @ the airport.

Are criminal because they have nothing in mind –
   & Sordello's story?
       winds thru this labyrinth
shot from both sides – or not shot
    Rise wall as Herod intended –
      and as for the Institut. Tien

命

not known & start 'is who is'
   there are such as
不 'der im Baluba das Gewitter gemacht hat'
知   when not of man, is of heaven
而   –
作 apparently they were sending it back
之 i.e. the petrol that wd have taken their cars to
者   Alessandria
我
是 也   (d'Egitto)
sold 7 ways cross wise. betrayer
   & hyper-betrayed
& Edda floated around in the waters
   along with the other nurses
ready for anything 'Tranne nella casa del re'
These words heard the bar room
     Rapallo
Manes. Manes. –
  Deus est Amor.
and @ Mt Segur they left not even the stair
Mithra est amor.

   were like the 2 halves of a seal
the two parts of a tally stick

the sun's lance measures the years
Young Filoppan clicked his heels
  bowed and offered the
    Bhgvad Ghita (in the original)

志
行
平
中
國
若
合
符
節

bought from the concierge who cd not
   (it wd seem) deliver the apartment house
save temporarily – nor the workers
pleased to be sold out like cattle –
   all their past gains wiped off in the flurry –
with the old joke about materia prima –
ripristinated – etcetera   as per 1919–1920

sd. the Reverend Cavallon Dottore – the Profs paid the banditi –
   et sic in saecula saeculorum –
one gang of ploots or another will hire Italian assassins
            in saecula saeculorum. the tomb of Theodoric
the mosaic in St. Apollinare classe
the tomb of Galla Placidia. Monreale
of St Apollinare called la nuova,
   an altar not in the chancel –
but the greeks move as a zodiac
in front of their solarist altar
these things are established   歲
Der im Baluba das Gewitter gemacht hat
& they drew the antelope in the sand
   & pierced same with a drawn arrow
& the next day @ dawn effaced same
   with prayer to the father of antelopes

this day as a 1000 years
never more now than at present

they have made their billions of profits
let them withdraw
不
以   private gain is not prosperity
利   equity is the treasure of states
為
利   III.2 son of heaven in bland splendour as
義   white sun upon grain field
為   over the ordered assembly.

& our tomorrow shall be as today
   & yet more sweet

Old Fordie quoting Cristina
   Be the fat man remembered
for his clarity – for the best of his writing
   gesta amicorum – gesta hominum
      de nos jours
who better – who was more constant? –
      neither Hardy nor Hudson –
the fallen   write him
     'à la realité du monde?'
yes, that is just what I have believed in –
à la realité – and coherence ?
     coherence.
Grüss Gott. 'God save you'   歲
in 'Spring & Autumn' there are no righteous wars
the wind also is of the process

you who have gone to the brink remember me
   & over, you have gone over
I cd. not save you
   & you are come into mind,
in the labyrinth. & I cd. not save you
nor find you a thread of issue.
   the wind also is of the process.
chi crescerà i nostri amori –
  but the augment? half the width of a sword's edge
tornai indietro a riguardare il passo.
  the drought also is of the process – shantih
& in that plain of
  Carpaccio?
    the skull, & dry bones
andai in Paradiso
     e passai per questa landa
Deus est amor,
   with the mind beaten down under its hatches
pitiless as the dog star
to the left of la bella torre the tower Ugolino

Ed ascoltando al leggier mormorio,
as I was listening to the enchanted song
there came new subtlety of eyes within my tent
whether of spirit or hypostasis
                              of glad hilarities,
saw no entire face
    but what the blindfold hides
            or at carneval
nor any pair showed anger
but as unaware of other presence
    smiled, each pair as at loveliest
Saw but the eyes & stance between the eyes,
    colour, diastasis,
                nor any pair showed anger
            as at other presence
    or careless or unaware it had not the whole tent's space,
nor was there space that a full *eidos* wd have taken
    how?
but if every soul lives in its own
    & proper space, & each of these
can penetrate and interpass
    as light thru light
casting but shade beyond the other lights
nor lose its forms, each soul
    keeping its cosmos,
    interlaced, free passing,
    that can cross & intercross

[as these were masks not masks
but had their loveliest life,
    six pair
nor was that all,
      but certainty.]

    sky's clear
    night's sea
    green as of mountain pool
    shone from the unmasked eyes in half-mask's room.
What thou lovest well
    shall not be reft from thee
What thou lovest well, remains,
      the rest is dross
What thou lov'st well is thy true heritage,

Whose world, or mine or theirs . . .
         or is it of none.

So, thinking of Althea at the grates,
two rose like lips pressed down upon my own

1st came the seen, then thus the palpable
elysium, tho' it were in the halls of hell.
What thou lovest well is thy true heritage
What thou lovest well shall not be reft from thee
What thou lovest remains, the rest is dross.

Yet from my tomb such flame of love arise
that whoso passes shall be warmed thereby;
           let stray cats curl there
                    where no tomb stone is
& girls' eyes sparkle, at the unmarked spot
let rancours wane
           & a slow drowse of peace pervade who passes.

Night rain and a Biddle sky
'That somewhat obstinate expression
            not devoid of amusement
on John Adams' face in his frontispiece
and that this might have to do with the question of funding'
'funding', as in the jargon of that epoch.

'H-how old is it?
                    How high is it? – eh?
Wu-what makes it a wonder?'
        La Torre di Pisa
in the dim mind of the sick-call
            The 'dark forest' (Turgenev's)   la selva . . . .

or a sky as of feldspar in autumn
when the sun goes to his rest

and to you Father Ascreus commen –
            about the time of my birthday
2 friends, new friends:
            this lady-bug not red brown but yellow
black spotted who draws in her head like a turtle
and this wasp yellow-banded
            aux yeux fleur-de-tête
in extacy over my jam-spread
            exuberant as a puppy-dog
and to Γεα the munificent
            my thanks for 2 most delicate mushrooms

while at next dawn with rain
          under the long line of gibbets
the lights of the punishmment area
          as some Jersey City by Lethe
plus my apologies to Hugo, via 'Bartlett':

 'Bees gather honey as the soul gathers light.'
Augurellus: Flos collegit rerum. Nov. 2.
My mind is stretched to the bursting point
          with this enormity
with the continuity of the gun-sales
What bird cries in November after the rain?

INCIPIT VITA NUOVA:
                              Tea at Norah's
and then @ the air-port:
          'what shall we do? We have no officers'.
And @ Settebagni nothing to pay for good bread –
          that after Roma –
nothing to pay for that egg
or those grapes
    or that double minestra
'Cosa fanno a Roma?'
          Wd/ I stay for the night,
and the first day they kept their packs
    and the second got rid of
          all military impedimenta
in fact of *all* impedimenta
          ready to escape in their underwear.
One night under the stars
          one on a bench at Rieti –
one on Bologna platform
    after food at the cab-driver's friend's trattoria
Lo sfacelo, understood why 'Hem' had written,
that is, 'his values'.

So that it must be almost clear
          to even the simple of heart
That if you spend ten billion

buying @ 35 dollar
instead of @ 21.60
        there will be 4 billion velvet
Some of which may have gone to Mocatta
        (Muscovites also selling)
   though our Treasury has no official knowledge
of anyone save the last firm that had it
        before the Treasury purchase
        and in June '39
I was told 'Oh, no' in Greenwich Connecticut
Oh no, they (that is Eden and Churchill)
are going to get into the government
in order to get the war started
        So why stop at Standard Oil and von Schröder
on account of a minor ὕστερον πρότερον?

And as reply, Stalin's:
           'I will believe the American'
           @ Winston's last public performance

So there was the gold, an' the silver
and the needlessness of the loans
        and I recalled that at a certain point of the conversation
I had said:
        'Good God / you don't mean
         they are worse than the other gang?'
and he (Borah) replied rather slowly: N - o - o
I wdn't/ say that but
        I can't work with 'em.

And years later it was, at least to some
        quite apparent
           that if the Treasury made the loans
instead of the private lenders
the interest wd/ accrue to the Treasury
and diminish by its amount the need of national taxes
        Mr Borah was never considered a safe man
           in certain quarters

verso la sera when a man throws a 40 ft. shadow

our Pisan sky making blue all the puddles
then the cloud hill rising over the rock range
                    quadrupling it
and the S.E. is a slit of fire

                    11th November
            So the Old Emperor said to Shun
舜
Shun   the emphasis is ideogramicly
                        on the lower component

'if you can keep the peace between
            those two hell-cats
you will have no trouble in running the Empire.'

Magnanimity/ magnanimity /
        I know I ask a great deal

Gaudier and Hulme gone in that one
Young Dolmetsch and Angold in this one

            and the Italians
                'are not interested
                in fighting foreigners,
they are only interested in fighting each other'
Olga Rudge dixit, who knows 'em

and it might have been avoided if
        Joe Davis had gone to Berlin instead of to Moscow

                'in our time
Give to us Peace'

(repeat here in Russian from the old Russian anthem
        'Give to us peace in our time, O Lord')

If the hoar frost grip thy tent
Thou wilt give thanks when night is spente.

Italy, my Italy, my God! my Italy
Ti abbraccio, o terra santa.

Black boy says
'Ah doan want to [miss] that psychiatrist'

The year dies and the camp falls apart.

        not in Cantos   14? nov

    without autosuggestion
    have found the soul inside the large intestine
    & consciousness that dark and turgid river
    upwelling from a clogged Plutonick liver

Montanari! young Dolmetsch,
      & that boy in the tank corps
reading Confucius. & when
the moon is not, count the night
                by Orion

VII

Prosaic Verses

1950–1960

and my gt/ aunt's third husband
received in ms/ from a friend
       the 49th canto –
you do not HSIN JI dip twice in one stream
                  sd/ Ocellus

Ian had felt it: 'blown to pieces?' but some fellow
going along hobbledy, singing, totally out of his mind

'were afraid he (Eddie) wdn't, at the last minute,
                    sign the order for mobilization'.
'If they can get a single phrase
                    out of my telephoning
and twist it, make it a head line ... '
                    thus the Rome correspondent
                            of the great London daily.

'Not judge my father' (Joinville)
        'he staved it off 18 years'.
    citoyen versus dictatorship

fell back on assassination, as per Fieschi, July 1835

        is not belief, it is conduct   德   tê ²⁻⁵
                                    with a circumflex
'But what will they DO?' wrote the Italian,
        'Connie Mack, Happy Chandler without an ideology
                to oppose that of the bolcheviki?'
        et les commères
            americaines avec leurs voix
                            impubères?

killed off in the first three months of it, 1914
        thus changing the english LANGUAGE
            Genlis says Chas II tried to restore it
'No Boldini, not me, you can paint my dog'
        sd/ Judith Gautier
   a question of values, the result used to hang
under a great red and gilt plank from the far orient

but the height of our paideuma, per Brancusi
        saying: One of those days when
            I wd/ not have given 20 minutes of my time
                    for anything under heaven.

An Aphrodite called PRAXIS
        a gate whereon stand lions
Circuits of large unhewn stones inside which
        perform the ritual DEMETRI Δημήτρι
        HIERA DROSIN APORRETA ἱερὰ δρῶσιν ἀπόρρητα
Ἀπόλλωνος Λυκίου
'An' the world is furious with me because I mean to keep peace'
                Sebastiani, re/ Belgium, 1831
The Spiritual Head came to contract a loan with the Rothschild
        Papal State ghetto abolished in 1850

'aint no son of a bitch can help me'
          remarked colleague Wiley
'Gawd's the only sonofabitch can help ME'
      'Slowness is beauty' sd/ Binyon.
That is to say: news that stays news
      'These peoples shd/ be like fratelli' sd/ Tcheou
'they read the same books'
              and Chas wrote:
  there is a red beetle that crawls about milk-weed
if you pick him up and hold him in yr/ closed hand
      he will sing to you. (Barnegat)
  one does not finish, wrote Humboldt to Agassiz
England has never hesitated to counterfeit
      professional pacifists will never tackle the problem
        of 'issue' L.s.d. issue
  will say anything, positively ANYthing, to keep discussion off 'issue'

grazia, that is: bellezza in motion
        ῥεῖ   not mere flow down a drain
phullotaxis

'one god and Mahomet' stamped by Roger of Sicily,
          on others a phallic sign
Offa's coins in Marcia   had arabic on 'em
                  and Marco Polo was jailed
Drove out not 12 Gods, but Augustus
                    aram
                       vult
                          nemus
                  That I wd/ put an altar
                                in every grove
              Gea, Tellus, DeMEter,
                          Phoibos, Selene,
My parenthesis is not like Henry's
            Giotto's circles, or whoso's in Pisa
that were in the Holy Field, many faces, wings whirling
        at first sight were but circular
                  may be Orcagna's
Mongol and briton both knew arab coin

John Heydon, the signatures,
                    and that plants migrate (dracoena)
pearls of Cubagna to Bruges fair, and Augsburg
            toward evening a purple reflection
                    plus a diaphana
                            alcatras, egrets, flamingoes

a bad thing to have an abstract idea of a senator,
            worse for a writer, but a bad thing for anyone

and Julian kept down the taxes,
            otherwise Ammianus not very lively
all men have senses, but not in the same degree
αἰσθάνεσθαι
Χρεία   necessity, as per Ellendt
            desire for a necessity

these statements are heteroclite? Life is heteroclite,
            crystals of like nature attractive
                    and a pattern, a situation,
in quella parte, a locus, indefinite middles
            not logic, nor indefinite media of exchange
                    αἰσθάνεσθαι
'Aesthetes' sd/ Marianne 'without sensibility'
            also 'that must be Mr Matthiessen (Christy)'
                    sd/ Marianne at the ball game.

The fact has a locus, it is not in vacuo.
        it exists in fact amid jumble
        which is not to say you may always neglect it
bad writers are without curiosity

'daily exercise or more power than any President'
                    Biddle to Cooper May 8 '37
Webster ... has no personal friends
   (earlier: Mr W. has not been refreshed)
sad and sour   and banks contracting
   grass crop always springing up fresh

     tuan   端

       and the four tuan
the foundations, the build-ups and reach-downs

   'certain specific acts (central government)
      are limited for great national purposes'
            Monroe-Cumberland road bill.
'any goddam politician can horn in and keep the war dangling'
              Stilwell Oct '44
'not expressly granted, cannot by implication'
                     A. Jxn
      hence Mr Landor's 'Ode'

Juan Ramon has flattened out and Ivan S. taken to farming

Now I remember that you built me a special gorilla-cage
          and that the foetor of Roosevelt
                    stank thru the shitpile that succeded him

moon bright like water

water like sky
usury, monopoly, changing the currency
                              METATHEMENON
            and exceeding, a falling short (of demand XREIA)

chih (4)   志

            directio voluntatis

The EMPEROR ploughed his furrow and his wife
        cared for the silk worms

as in the Law Hall of Poictiers, proportion.

        shall the san kōu   三孤   kōu

lose their tradition?   孝
or the Zauberflöte have no meaning
hsiao⁴   t'ang¹   湯
        tzu⁴   自
        ko ²⁻⁵   葛   1766 ante Xristum
opened the coppermine
        λαμπρὰ συμβαίνει   some narrow rat
                                hunting the ark
                                on Mt Arrarat.

yellow leaves withered
        till beasts fed upon men
as a great rose brushing my eyelids
        e dica cala non dica converso
      貞 chên in every case
                    οἱ βάρβαροι very destructive
      能   meng²
      以
      衆   chung⁴   by collaboration
There is no doubt that Mencius is, here & there,
                    very laconic

for a word / for the mistranslation of XREIA
        for 'creates' shd/ read 'participates'

and as Beddoes said: waiting
      gibbering for a definition   五
wu³ shih²⁻⁵ i³ hsueh²⁻⁵ i⁴   十
                           以
                           學
                           易
said En Bertrans
            'hack down my trees'
                       repeat, Pittigliano.
even Sowbelly, when younger, thought of reforestation
and Luigi, gobbo, made his communion,
             peddler's pack over hillside,   宜
                with wheat grain at mass time

L'arif est gai, de bonne humeur, souriant
without this hilaritas Xtianity fell
i.e. fell when it lost it; if it lost it
                    jews had it in that sinagogue, in Gibraltar
pusillanimous wanting all men cut down to worm-size
            Mencius, Dante, Agassiz
                            qualify
'easier to convert 'em after they're fed'
                (pup or someone to Augustine)
Varsovie, Avril, pour defendre sa devise
                    i $^{1-5}$ 一
                    yen^2 言
                    fên^4 償
                    shih^4 事

一   i$^{1-5}$
人   jên^2
定   ting^4
國   kuo$^{2-5}$

Stella and Jaime from cancer, old Wyndham gone blind.
in the Dead Sea, potassium chloride, magnesium chloride
allume di Tolfa, Spanish alum vurry historic
                and that gold, bait is chaos, is against all civic order
Sarah lay with Sathanas   ??qt Mussato
        to bring forth the Ace of Toads.
    But the stone pulpit in the Piazza (Brescia)

showed voluntatem, showed a potenza
he asked, and received, a ventennio

When the dancing girls left the temples, the religion fell in decay
        ihr Tochter von Hierusalem
                Aug/ Boeckh on Athens, at last mentions Salmasius.
                ?for the last time in an hundred years

'as to why that polish wumman never stuck a knife into him'
                elderly congressman trying to figger it out, many years later
                        donkey boys singing Hafiz, in Teheran
colder the winter, stronger the wheat   che ge-ge-germoglia
        Iron at Clazomenae
republic (Athens) did not adulterate the/
and the susceptible Pilsudsky decorated Stephanska's sister
        right thru her robe, onto her buzzom

                chlorides, the dead sea
Truth not enough but
                義   needed in praxis
we are historians
                foglie d'autunno
Art is local 地 sd Vlaminck

Marie Walpurge   1749
        progres, coton, de bazin,
cuirs de Russie, cut the salt tax de Bohême
'Europe exhausted' sd/ Picabia 'by the conquest of Alsace-Lorraine'

autarchia at least for silk-manufacture
        (Marie Walpurge)

Byng licked by Galissonnière
        Joseph second ploughed his imperial furrow
        this is Austria, Habsburg

a road still in Belgium d/ 1780 Maria Theresa
        her thalers still in Addis Abeba
                Britich made fake Maria Theresas

tax reform, vivres à moins de frais
Fromageot, Prieur-Comandataire, Lord of Ussel,
                                   recording
in her time was Mozart;
          freed serfs who wd/ fight frogs and Prussians

Jovis stella, Antoninus, Theresa, and Chlodwig
              in her time was Culloden
Maria mi fé, Gentz et Metternich me disfecerunt
             'chi stima l'onore assai'
damn brits brought in hrooshunz after Bergen-op-zoom
Maria Theresa cut down taxes   1748

          lin, chanvre, law-suits inside one year
de coton, de bazin,
                  end of Bohemian salt tax

an old adultery still shedding rose leaves
                Yvanoe Ferrara's name, murmured Hovey
                    or was it Carman

'Est deus in nobis'
         hilaritas of the aarif, Good Humour, J. Adams

                信 hsin⁴
                中 chung

Old Peters after '48 that was,
        escaped over the desert and for the first time
        noticed stars
hence the little observatory disused in upper N. York state
        Savant à peine qui fut Talleyrand
But above all sd/ Bismarck 'not start a war
                by breaking a treaty'
to make debt and profit dealers in that 'commodity'

一
言
債
事

an old tree in Connecticut
        where Kit Wadsworth
Bismarck saw war wd knock off 3 emperors

mit das Bankhaus Pacelli kompromettiert
        so Sarti was elected

Erigena, Gemisto, Intorcetta

So that Fordie wd/ dress himself up like Marschall von Bieberstein
        in Bülow's Memoirs, and with me in an old velvet coat
wd/ charge out into whatever drawing-room wd/ admit him
        that I might observe, I suppose, the there fauna,
            neben der Kunst des Hippokrates
Solari remembered, 1943, a cavalry charge, thought it the last one

                                        in history, when they
broke thru the Ausstrians in, was it November 1919? 1918?

a little Vernunft on our side wd/ be desirable
                    Porphyrogennetos   (question n doubled?)
Le bûcheron américain
          Ne s'intéresse à rien. Talleyrand
          Il n'a de souvenir à placer nulle part

                    Bellum cano perenne
Alexander to Blackstone, Maria Theresa, von Humboldt
          the water-bugs mittens in shadow
that is particulars, as Roscoe's 'Lorenzo' page 2,7,7, Bohn
          'transferring their own burthens to . . .
                                        their posterity'
indenting the Victorian mind, perhaps as deeply as the bug's mits
          the wet rock beneath him
come in un botro, sd/ Pea (pronounced peh-ah, not pea)

novis, nova remedia
Cerutti: they cannot think anything noble
Out of chrysalis
                    bright antennae
2 Jan/
Wings like feldspar
                    & how strong the grip on your finger
to maintain their wing-spread
            Margaret, Ingeborg in congedo.
would stand only 9th mid the 70/
                    this stone giveth sleep

spruce, juniper, coral
                    you will find in these mountains
snow stretch above valleys
            Rock's land and Goullart's
copper and coral for sale there,
                    but years?
                            no years on sale in that market
air blown into word-form
14th dec. '57
            ½ pie of the moon in the morning crispness
                    snow-coloured
above a puffed and perched starling
(confirmed by the Boyd-Henderson calendar)
in green for the light here   in emerald
                    the body of jade

the wide wing spread
from pole, in saeculorum
    to their proper island, living on milkweed
farfalla,
        3000 miles from the pole,
                        yearly returning
       Laval, Pétain, gli onesti
             yet till they be brought to Les Invalides
Saunderson wouldn't stand it
             and went 'into the City'
(re Mihaelovitch)
Gaudier for that turn of a shoulder
             a forméd trace in the mind

Till Di Marzio cita:
The Eparch, Melek, the Sheng Yu, Coke and Demeter,
Cita: ragion civile, a liquidity
                    and that friends are the treasure,
never with books alone, la scuola is il fare, the doing,
                    1482–1540, Ser Guicciardini,
Firenze, that mutation begets mutation,
                                        Modena, Reggio, Parma
a republic coordinate, and against barbari and the preti,
even great princes are short of ambassadors,
    and let them keep out of commerce,
'no rule can cover all cases
                    one day at a time'
                                        Guicciardini,
That Florence will undo the mount, or the mount
                    will polish off Florence,
        'o Firenze disfarà el monte',
and showed dislike of analogies
                        'not expect folk will follow your novelties',
            Ducunt volentes fata,
injure no man,
        Adams to Jefferson, 'you fear the one, I, the few'.
An Italy free of barbarians.
And as for the Medici, my father wanted 'em let back as privates,
                and not to try *fuori tempo*
have always desired, naturally,
                    the ruin of the ecclesiastical state.

and as for who can neither do nor keep silent,
                         equalitarian, seething with envy.
Sacramentum proborum,
                         hominium de visneto,
justice neither sold nor delayed.

rumours, blown words under Li Chiang,
                         these words in the snow range,
in the mirroured hall amid images,
non usurabit, even if it falls back to the monarch,
                         law english, Welsh of the Marca.
Mr. Biddle's 3 nut shells, Webster, Clay and Calhoun.
   until specie is required for export
'Not the leading element, property is not, in society',
that was Johnson, Andrew, and Mr. Quigley said:
         'If he, Del Mar, were a great historian
               I would have heard of him'.
Birds are not, said Huddy, automata.
                         and the early romans cd/ not 'take' satire.

                         ga dara agdu

Durandus (St Pourçain) that
                         particulars are higher than abstract.

大
學   ta seu,
端   this part is for adults,

a basis, and consuetudo
   yet if all usurpations   pass into custom,
Anselm, Ford, Talleyrand, Bülow.
& that quite simple men reach the Snow Range,
         Cerutti indignant: 'cannot think anything noble'
The akasa, if that's what they call it / recorded.

Out of Earth into tree
          then '*cervo*'
There is a tree in the stag's horns
There in the East
                    was Orion
His stars are now in mid-heaven
The stag's moon begets Actaeon

          Daughter of a sun-priest
in Babylon
                    Julia Domna
Μέμνονι 'Ηῴῳ
    ψυχὴ ἀθάνατος
. . .

& that greek Perigrinus
          built his own pyre –
ou tis.
    never can remember his name
the fire flies are
          yellow green in the twilight
. . .

'We have not used the
          wrong names for objects'
moon light white as a bone

will turquoise see from yr eyeballs
or silver teeth

           give you laughter.
her face white as the cliff side
the water blue like her eyes

And might be lost if I do not record them
                              If I record them?
Essad, Essad Bey, 'Secrets of Caucasus' 12 of them
Life of Stalin.
Der Weg stirb, wrote (quoted) Frobenius
Albert Londres was not read, is not,
          La Chine en Folie, Au Bagne, Dante n'a rien . . . et cetera
and the inscription,
                    did I say Hammurabi, why did I get it Hammurabi
                                                      Hymur?
at Behistun? Remy out of print,
          and, naturally Willy,
                              the trivia of an era.

Waddell, Rock, Goullart says some tribes die out.
and pronounces it Nashi, against Rock's obvious spelling.
          go to Rawlinson
And that history is of 'issue',
          i.e., the power to issue the currency.
                    Bellum perenne.
a subject.   (this can be
                              FINIS, if necessary)

one at a time, to judge men,
                    judge ideas.
and the system, not the rate, of taxation.
the relative honesty of the courts, that was Persia,

                    vide Rawlinson.
Nuissance to outlive one's intelligence
            with the young waiting a synthesis.
PANTA HREI / we are not faced with a stasis.
Faruk sold out the museum.
                    Brancus was against 'monumental'
'Nous sommes dedans quelque chose'
            Was it Pasteur he worked with.
And they run after a train that has gone.
Wyndham Lewis took blindness,
                        rather than have his mind stop.
let the drill whirl, there is, yes: repetition.
Who defied hell & the lightnings
                & ends like a sick mouse on a rubble heap.
Who again went down into hell
                into cowardice, dither and death fear
here hell the inferno –
                but for the going forth
                        by day
                                the going –
That the forces of evil are vanquished –
They have for the moment,
                        thrown their last throw.
Conquers
        who conquers,
Cristo Re
        Dio Sole
        the Erynnis
The trees in mist hold their beauty
I have been a pitiless stone –
                        stone making art work
and destroying affections.
in meine Heimat
            Kam ich wieder
where the dead walked & the living were
                            made of cardboard

                    ————

            (scene shift)

Till suddenly the tower
                 blazed with the light of Astarte
@ Genova the port lay below us.
Miracolo di Dio
              ch'amor riceve
                       né la calunnia
                              né l'invidia te toca.
Serena, neither pride nor pretentions to ownership move thee.

the madness & cancer are nothing
the suffering is not vicarious.
one dies without saving the world –
& with Seneca: no gods in this
                              part of sky space

MA LA BELLEZZA ESISTE

Delcroix thought it (the suffering) was vicarious –
'Carry the blindness':
              one out of so many
Mist hides the trees.
it now hides the great valley.
& Tchou Yin's cord comes to the surface –
Like brothers –
        they ought to be –
                  these two peoples
his little brother marked down
   seen from a bus
outside porta del Popolo
              is the debacle –
How confess error
& not cleave to some fallacy
by that confession –
somewhere in the snarl is a tenderness
I wd look on you, dying
I shall not, we have self'd ourselves out of the world.

But this is not *atasal*
obviously this is not *atasal*
& I have spelled it correctly –
& his Eminence is correct
        in pointing out that hell
                cannot be merely external
a chocolate cream world
If evil mere absence of good?
Morir –
    ma nel labirinto
                della morte –
più lungo ritrovarti
In the labyrinth of
        death longer to
                find you –
& the rivets of tyranny
        driven over our head
'the portal to inquisition'
                Thiers
Tragic heart, they have
        flayed your compassion
there is no cave left in the world
there is no shelter
what flower is come
        in the hedgerow
the white bud half open

To have seen you walk
        in flat shoes
            & have let you go
                this is agony
or seated in your flower-skirt
                under elm trees.
Troica Roma resurges
These are the failures –
aged gem Fasa –
That the city be
        there in the mind –
Tragic heart once given

when separation is
                    crucifixion
& light is in meeting.

Dec. 5. 4 p.m.   Pax.
These sudden devaluations
always more somewhere
                    than elsewhere
Threats of devaluation
keeping the nerves raw
        by scaring the market
sweeping away the life's fruit
in an instant
    or over a week end
100 million dashed into slavery.
lure of the luxury trades.
drugs to break courage.

for the blind mice
        of the nations –
women starved
        with brutality
                    envy

But the sense
        of awe is
            not vanity
    the bright moment
            not vanity

before I died
    I had & given
these hours

VIII

Lines for Olga

1962–1972

Domenica

& the grasshopper was not yet dead on his stalk,
& her flame prolonged him
          as it had with the dragon fly
invicta.
          & that she would not relinquish hope
& that here was a will to go on living
despite all betrayals,
                    sero   sero
That she could not believe in such perfidy.
& Rossaro sd/ the honest man
          can not believe the mascalzone etc.
he the *onesto*
          does not see the other man's evil
till it surprises him

The gondolas dying in
                    their sewers
& the grasshopper dead
                    on his stalk

& she, Olga, with serene
                    courage
bearing it all
   finding beauty
   where the last
       vestige of it
       still was,
   finding it in the least items
       & in the great
       in San Marco
       & the piazza
               by night.

hers the heroism to build upon sand

and as to why this
                timing?
Olga ever willing
    to resurrect the good,
        such as it was
            that was in me

& the signs clustering
        ever increasing
cumulation of evil
        against us,
minute clusters of symbols

the real poem is her poem
She wrote her Eurydice

saw beauty & showed it
against my distraction

to sunset and the cherry-tree

if there was beauty she saw it

    & lifted the weight
& I have profaned

flood & flame
thru the long years
          by night & hill path
great courage in frail frame
toughened by four decades
of climbing thru dark
                    on hill paths,
knowing each stone
almost as if by name

from eyes' gleams
          ∩ ∩
Ode,
          like an old love.

But against mounting evils
she held the will toward good
Her clear lucidity
that she saw the Duce with level eyes

Olga's name being courage
         And the delicacy of her insight,
Her name being fidelity
         and the sensitivity of her fingers;
For the delicacy of her perception
         for the fineness of her memory
         of every beautiful thing she had seen.

For the contrejour of her with her violin
         and the beach at Sta Margherita
                  the year she was there with Lindy.
For the walk lungoSenna
         For the evening at Ville D'Avray
For her perception of people

                                        Ezra

Festa di San Pantaleo

And there was nothing but water melon
                    at the top of Mt Chocorua
& she tried to sell her Hans Andersen picture book
            with the red gilded cover
                                to the janitor
& she left the school picnic
to follow a funeral
& had no arbre de Noël
& she was beautiful on the beach @ Sta Margherita
& the mill race ran level our table at Ville Davray
& she was beautiful as la Mousmé
& she climbed the rope ladder over ship side –

& her name was courage
& she had pity for every living thing
& kept me alive for ten years
            for which no one will thank her
her red heart in flask of perfume

(*Thanksgiving Day*)

Notes

The uncollected texts presented in this volume follow the original publications as indicated, with occasional corrections. Scholars have studied and transcribed Ezra Pound's drafts and notebooks, and I make use of their transcriptions and reproductions as indicated in these Notes. Previously unpublished texts are in the Beinecke Rare Book and Manuscript Library at Yale University (Pound Papers, Rudge Papers, and additions). Unless otherwise noted, I have followed Pound's inconsistent punctuation and spelling. However, I have made a few silent corrections and regularized Greek words and phrases. The Notes do not attempt an exhaustive account of references and allusions, but provide an overview and elucidate some details, especially information not available in reference works like Carroll F. Terrell's ground-breaking *Companion to the Cantos of Ezra Pound* (University of California Press, 1984).

References to *The Cantos of Ezra Pound* are to the 1995 New Directions paperback edition, and follow canto/page format; e.g., 46/231 = canto 46, p. 231. In the earlier hardbound collected New Directions edition (1970) and in the uniform 1976 edition issued by Faber in hardback and paperback, cantos 74 to 117 have lower (by twenty) page numbers. Thus, for example, a citation given below as 74/445 will be found in British and US editions of the 1970s at 74/425, while 51/251 remains the same in all volumes. This discrepancy is due to the fact that in later US editions cantos 72–73 were added at pp. 423–442.

I. THREE CANTOS: LONDON 1915–1917

The text of 'Three Cantos', the first finished version of the beginning of Pound's long poem, is reprinted here from *Poetry* (June, July, and August 1917). Pound slightly revised these cantos for publication in *Lustra* (Knopf, 1917). He recast them entirely in 1923 for *A Draft of XVI Cantos* (1925). See Miles Slatin, 'A History of Pound's Cantos', *American Literature* 35 (1963), pp. 183–95, and Ron Bush, *The Genesis of Ezra Pound's Cantos* (Princeton UP, 1976).

Hang it all, there can be but one Sordello! (p. 3)
Pound alludes to Browning's *Sordello*, a notoriously obscure long poem that has found few readers. *The Cantos* often refer to the troubadour Sordello of Mantua (who figures importantly in Dante's *Purgatorio*) and to his sometime lover Cunizza da Romano (and her brother Ezzelino). The debate with Browning about the possibility of writing a new *Sordello* is briefly recapitulated at the beginning of the final version of canto 2. Displaying his greater familiarity with the troubadours, Pound criticizes Browning for his anachronisms, while admitting that poetry and history need not always agree. He goes on to describe his pleasant retreat on Lake Garda, at Sirmione, the home of Catullus, and recalls having sat penniless in Venice on the steps of the old Custom House ('Dogana') – a vignette eventually placed at the beginning of canto 3. This is followed by further idyllic images of Lake Garda ('bright gods and Tuscan'), Oriental landscapes, evocations of Guido Cavalcanti (with an allusion to Boccaccio's story about Guido – *Decameron* 6.9), and musings on Botticelli's Venus and its model (Simonetta Vespucci). All of this, Pound tells us, is part of his 'phantastikon', a sort of transparent sphere of images that he carries about with him. Casella is the musical friend whom Dante encounters in *Purgatorio* 2.76–133.

Leave Casella (p. 9)
Pound's reminiscences proceed from Sordello's Mantua to the Provence of the troubadours, to his friend Arnold Dolmetsch (maker of rare instruments, celebrated by Gabriele D'Annunzio, among others), to a paraphrase from the Chinese, set against Catullus's famous version of Sappho. Pound recalls poetic visions that he encountered in the Dordogne and on Salisbury Plain (the latter revis-

ited in 80/535), and some love stories from old Provence (implying that nothing changes). He goes on to the Cid's exile (cf. 3/11–12), Camões's Inês de Castro (to be treated at length in canto 30), and the relations between Portugal and the Netherlands – all of which he had discussed in *The Spirit of Romance*. This anthological canto closes with the object lesson of a failed contemporary artist who chose to return to the US rather than 'beat out his exile' (as Pound has happily done).

Another's a half-cracked fellow – John Heydon (p. 16)
John Heydon was a seventeenth-century quack alchemist and astrologer, known to Pound through Yeats. Heydon does not appear in the revised cantos 1–3, but resurfaces many years later in cantos 87 and 91. Always attracted by heterodox visionaries, Pound proceeds to summon the Florentine Platonists and Lorenzo Valla, whose love of the Latin tongue he obviously shares. He then offers a 'rough' rendering of a Latin version of *Odyssey* 11, the work of one Andreas Divus, printed in 1538 together with a translation by 'a certain Cretan' of the Homeric *Hymns*. In his essay 'Early Translators of Homer' Pound recalls picking up Divus's *Odyssey* on a Paris quay. His translation at second hand of Odysseus's descent to Hades, written in a style reminiscent of alliterative Anglo-Saxon verse, accounts for the remainder of the canto, followed by a brief address to Divus (a footnote, as it were) and by quotations from the Cretan's *Hymns*, with a fragmentary evocation of 'golden' (*auream*) Venus. Pound was to use this Homeric pastiche, slightly abbreviated, as canto 1, i.e., as the symbolic overture to his ambitious new *Odyssey*.

'What do I mean by all this clattering rumble?' (p. 21)
Pound attempted several sequels to 'Three Cantos', but only in 1919 completed canto 4, which is more visionary and less discursive than 'Three Cantos', and is the first canto to survive mostly unchanged in the final version. The present fragment (c. 1917) picks up the familiar and self-questioning tone of 'Three Cantos' to argue that through poetry we may create for ourselves a more heroic life (citing Dante, *Paradiso* 1.70: 'no words could express transcendence of the human'). Pound praises his Vorticist associates Wyndham Lewis and Henri Gaudier-Brzeska, the young sculptor who died at the front in 1915. As suggested in the conclusion of 'Three Cantos' I, artwork like Lewis's series *Timon of Athens* is a more direct and uncompro-

mising expression of modernity than Pound's idyllic revisitations of literary scenes and landscapes. This fragment and the two that follow are transcribed and discussed in Christine Froula, *To Write Paradise: Style and Error in Pound's Cantos* (Yale University Press, 1993), pp. 74–75, 103, 104.

When you find that feminine contact (p. 23)
Manuscript, c. 1915. Omakitsu is the Japanese name for the Tang dynasty Chinese poet Wang Wei, see the epigraph for Pound's 'Four Poems of Departure' (*Cathay*). At about age thirty, Pound often wrote nostalgically of lost youth and premature old age, e.g., in 'Villanelle: The Psychological Hour'. The Latin words recall Horace's 'Eheu fugaces, Postume, Postume' (*Odes* 2.14).

What's poetry? (p. 24)
Excerpt from a typescript of seventy-one lines, c. 1915. Douglas Goldring (1887–1960), collaborator of Ford Madox Hueffer (Ford) and author of the fine memoir of Ford and his circle *South Lodge* (1943), published in *Poetry*, September 1914, the poem 'Calle Memo O Loredan' (the name of an actual alleyway, or *calle*, in Venice), beginning 'We were staying (that night) in a very old palace'. Pound speaks of poetry's evocative power. The gilded Venetian ceilings (glossed by Pound in a letter, see Carlo Izzo, *Civiltà americana* (1967), II, p. 256) recur in 3/20 ('the lit cross-beams'), 4/16 ('Gilt rafters' – again in conjunction with the mysterious three steps of Angoulême), and 74/482 ('and the gilded cassoni'). The cloister of St Trophime in Arles, unspoiled by usury, is extolled in 45/230.

II. PARIS 1920–1922

And So shu stirred in the sea (p. 27)
Typescript draft for the opening of a 'Canto VII', which after many revisions became canto 2 of the final version. The typescript contains numerous corrections in longhand (not reproduced here), which were incorporated in later drafts (see below). So-shu is a Chinese projection of the Poundian poet who summons images from the waves. Pound reflects on the nature of visionary experiences and identifies with the prehistoric artists of Les Eyzies in Périgord. St Theresa's

vision is recalled in Pound's 'Postscript to the "Natural Philosophy of Love" by Remy de Gourmont' (1921) and in 87/593. The crystal sphere, first described in 'Three Cantos' I, recurs in cantos 27 and 116. The draft continues with a description of Poseidon and Tyro's love-making in the sea, and with a northern landscape of seabirds and seals, that appear with revisions in all versions. Tyro (wife of Creteus, son of Aeolus, hence 'Aiolides') is one of the fair ladies whom Odysseus meets in Hades (see above, 'Three Cantos' III: *Another's a half-cracked fellow*). Her lovemaking with Poseidon is sketched on the basis of *Odyssey* 11.235–52 – see especially the wave's 'wall' that conceals the lovers, and the god's salutation to the young woman: Χαῖρε, γύναι, φιλότητι . . .'. The birds that bathe and extend their wings translate a line from the Old English poem *The Wanderer* (47: 'baþian brimfuglas, brædan feþra'); Pound cites line 15 in the original ('The weary spirit cannot withstand fate'). 'Three Cantos' III (later canto 1) had already correlated the Anglo-Saxon mariners with Homer's Odysseus.

Sudden gift of the stranger (p. 29)

This is the second typescript version of the beginning of 'Canto VIII' (later canto 2). It begins with a brief nostalgic lyric (dated 1919) and a reference to the Arab ghazal (usually an 8/10-line stanza with identical rhymes). There follow, from the previous draft, So-shu, Tyro's lovemaking (compacted) and the seabirds. (The spelling 'churrned' suggests pronunciation à la Yeats, as in Pound's own readings.) Then a new episode is announced: Acoetes's tale of the epiphany of Dionysus among the pirates who kidnapped him (from Ovid's *Metamorphoses* 3), which was to become the canto's main narrative.

Dido choked up with tears for dead Sicheus (p. 31)

These are the opening lines of 'Canto VIII' as it appeared in *The Dial*, May 1922. To continue from canto 7 (published August 1921 in the same review) Pound repeats the motif of inconsolable Dido (7/26–27) and transforms her into the languishing Muse awaiting a new singer (Pound) in a sensual Mediterranean setting. This passage was cancelled in 1923 when Pound incorporated most of 'Canto VIII' into what is now canto 2, adding at the beginning a brief version of the address to Browning from 'Three Cantos', and retrieving So-shu from the previous drafts, as reprinted above. To recapitulate, the order of subjects in the various versions is as follows:

1. So-shu – *visions* – *Les Eyzies* – Tyro – sea-birds – *lament for the disappearance of the god* – seal.

2. *Ghazel* – So-shu – Tyro – sea-birds – seal – Acoetes speaks of Dionysus.

3. *Dido and the widowed Muse* – *triremes at Cyprus* – (Tyro) – seal – long passage on Helen of Troy – Tyro – sea-birds – Acoetes and Dionysus.

In the final canto 2 the order is: Browning – Sordello – So-shu – seal etc. as in version 3. I have italicized subjects omitted in the final redaction.

By the arena, you, Thomas amics, Galla Placidia, and the Roman (p. 32)
From an early typescript draft of the Renaissance saga of Sigismondo Malatesta (cantos 8–11). Pound was in Verona in late May–early June 1922 with his friend Bride Scratton ('Ti') and T. S. Eliot, who was about to launch *The Criterion*. ('Bitter Bonomelli' was a popular spirit.) The Verona episode brings back the memory of another holiday shared with Eliot, in 1919 at Excideuil, birthplace of the troubadour Giraut de Bornelh. Pound reverted to these meetings with Eliot in cantos 29 and 78, and planted the refrain of the Verona Arena in cantos 4, 11, and 12 ('And we sit here. I have sat here / For forty four thousand years'). The gold shining in the gloom of the Mausoleum of Galla Placidia (Ravenna) recurs in cantos 11, 17, 21; the 'gonads in organdy' in 21/99. The Dante quotation from *Purgatorio* 26.148 was one of Eliot's touchstones, see the finale of *The Waste Land*. For a discussion of this significant draft and of its different versions see Peter D'Epiro, *A Touch of Rhetoric* (UMI, 1983), pp. 23–24, 47–48. On Pound and Eliot's 1922 meeting in Verona see Lawrence Rainey, *Ezra Pound and the Monument of Culture* (University of Chicago Press, 1991), pp. 54–57, 238–40; Stefano M. Casella, *Bollettino della Civica Biblioteca di Verona* 4 (1998–99), pp. 193–216; Rosella Mamoli Zorzi et al., *In Venice and in the Veneto with Ezra Pound* (Venice: Supernova, 2007), pp. 75–82.

III. RAPALLO AND VENICE 1928–1937

the new shoots rise by the altar (p. 37)
Manuscript draft for canto 47. Brackets indicate conjectural readings. Pound evokes the erotic rituals of Adonis by means of the 'new shoots'

(displayed in Italian churches on Maundy Thursday to symbolize the Holy Sepulchre, or '*sepolcri*') and the lights floated in Rapallo during the festivities of the Madonna of Montallegro (July 1–3). The latter is a very ancient custom that Pound interprets as a re-enactment of the death of Adonis, whose blood reddens the Mediterranean. For details and illustrations see *Paideuma* 14.2–3 (1985), pp. 179–209. The draft goes on to explore the mystery of the eternal female in a Homeric context (Circe), in the archaic language of cantos 45 and 47, associated with fertility and the curse of usury. Though the middle-aged poet seems to reduce woman to her genital apparatus (she only knows what she can touch with '2 spans'), in the end he remains puzzled and awed by her power and indebted to her for his creativity. Odysseus, son of Laertes, is called Laertiades by Homer. 'Moly', as in canto 47, is the magic herb which protects Odysseus from Circe's sorcery.

irritable and unstable (p. 39)

Three typescript pages with many longhand corrections not all of which are reproduced here. (For example, the line 'Titular head, be Pu Yi' is crossed out – Pu Yi, last emperor of China, abdicated in 1912; in 1932 he was installed by the Japanese as 'titular head' of the puppet state of Manchuko.) In preparation for the Ligurian rites of canto 47, Pound observes the hills and the sea of Rapallo and records episodes like the suicide of two lovers, but is chiefly enchanted by the rural natural world (cicadas and fireflies). He contrasts Liguria, land of the olive tree, with the land of wheat, and is thinking evidently of Stalin's Russia, which has abolished the sense of nature's sacredness (the ancient rites of Adonis, of which the Easter and summer celebrations in Rapallo are, he believes, a revival). (The contrast between Italy and Russia is anticipated in 27/130–31.) The opening lines were used in 37/185 and allude to Guido Cavalcanti's theory of love. The leopard men and the final Italian quotation ('Galileo was an ignoramus and brought imbecility to the world') appear in 48/241. Mark A. Carleton is the botanist who introduced Russian (Kubanka) wheat to America; he is mentioned again in connection with Italian grain rites in 80/533. Pound derived from Allen Upward the association of Sitalkas (a Thracian king) with ceremonial sacrifices (74/457, 78/499), as well as the theme of the two-coloured olive leaf associated with Athena 'glaukopos' and her owl (see above, 'Three Cantos' I: *Hang it all, there can be but the one 'Sordello'!*). In Pound's *Des Imagistes* anthology Upward is represented by a few prose poems, and H.D. by six lyrics, one of which is titled 'Sitalkas'. The quotation of Bion's *Epitaph of Adonis* 93–94 is used as a refrain in canto 47.

'Spent yesterday drawing a grasshopper' (p. 42)

Beginning of an early typescript draft of canto 49. Dorothy Pound was a gifted artist, see her book *Etruscan Gate* (Rougemont Press, 1971), which includes a drawing of a grasshopper. Canto 49, known as the 'Seven Lakes Canto' (published 1937), is a paraphrase of poems descriptive of a traditional Chinese region and landscape, hence the association with Dorothy's sketching.

'From this grotto' (p. 43)

This passage opens a second typescript draft of canto 49. It refers to a bilingual inscription placed in 1877 over the portal of the 'Grotta Byron' of Portovenere (near La Spezia, some thirty miles south of Rapallo): 'THIS GROTTO / WHICH INSPIRED LORD BYRON / IN THE SUBLIME POEM THE CORSAIR / RECORDS [sic] THE IMMORTAL POET / WHO / AS A DARING SWIMMER / FROM PORTOVENERE TO LERICI DEFIED THE WAVES OF THE LIGURIAN SEA'. Pound's typescript reads, 'This grotto, winch', and he never crossed out 'winch' (obviously a misreading of 'WHICH'), but he did add 'From' in longhand at the beginning, and this is the source of the edited text presented here. Henry James noted the inscription when visiting Portovenere (pronounced Portovènere) in 1877, and joked about the cult of Byron ('Italy Revisited' 3, in *Italian Hours*). Hence Pound's criticism of James's alleged inaccuracy and his defence of Byron's daring swimming. He associates Byron's legendary swim from Portovenere to Lerici with his celebrated crossing of the Hellespont, and refers to another favourite poet and swimmer, Swinburne (see also 82/543). Clearly Pound, a swimmer himself, is more partial to the athletic Byron and Swinburne than to the fastidious introvert James. The passage is fascinating because it presents Byron, James and Pound visiting in sequence the same mysterious grotto in a site associated with Venus (Porto-Venere). Its relation to the Chinese-Japanese landscape poetry of canto 49 is clear (the poet confronting the natural world and writing or sketching). Presumably Pound decided not to use this anecdotal introduction in order to preserve the immediacy of the Oriental vision. The phrase in old French, 'A quarante ans et force ma gourme jecté', reminiscent of (but not quoted from) François Villon, may be translated, 'At forty years of age and having perforce sown my wild oats'. It refers to Pound's age when visiting Portovenere in the late 1920s; compare his premature concern with the debilities of middle age (above, *When you find that feminine contact*), also Villon's 'En l'an trentiesme de mon aage' (quoted in *Hugh Sewlyn Mauberley*).

A dangle of fishermen's lanthorns (p. 44)
From a typescript draft for canto 49. Compare lines 1–8 with the published version (49/244–45). Of lines 9–31 Pound preserved only two lines of political diatribe (49/245). The digression opens with an image of Venice, where Pound regularly vacationed in summer, in fact near the Giudecca canal. The theme of the 'twice-born' (*digenes*, Pound's spelling of *digonos*) is obscurely evoked in cantos 48 and 74, see also above, *irritable and unstable*.

SHINES in the mind of heaven GOD (p. 46)
This passage and the five that follow (c. 1935) are drafts for canto 51 (the second 'usura' canto). Reproductions of the typescript are included in *Usura-Cantos XLV und LI: Texte, Entwürfe und Fragmente*, ed. Eva Hesse (Zürich: Arche, 1985), pp. 55–61. The opening lines are the same as in canto 51, with a quotation of Guido Guinizelli's celebrated canzone 'Al cor gentil', but here Pound stops to comment and repeat Guinizelli's phrase, the significance of which, he tells us, goes well beyond literary history (an 'affair for poltroons'). This still world of light is threatened by the 'bed bug' time, whose evil and destructiveness are also denounced in cantos 30, 49 and 74/464 ('Time is not, Time is the evil'). The passage closes with an anecdote about a séance with the ghost of Robert Browning, whose poem 'Bishop Blougram's Apology' offers the worldly bishop's defence against the critical young idealist Gigadibs. (Pound appears to conflate the two speakers, and misspells 'Blougram' as he had done in 'Mr Nixon' of *Hugh Selwyn Mauberley*.)

colla coda aguzza (p. 47)
A variation on the episode of the winged monster Geryon in *Inferno* 17 ('coda aguzza' is his 'sharp tail'), eventually reduced to a few lines at the close of canto 51. To Pound, Geryon is a symbol of usury, which is mightier than the sword (also with a sexual innuendo). All that

matters is the control of credit, a voice with a Jewish accent tells us, suggesting the stock identification of the usurer and the Jew, by which Pound, obsessed with his war against usury, is increasingly tempted. (The Jewish accent is imitated in a would-be humorous context in canto 35 ('Mitteleuropa') and recurs in the 1943 draft on Napoleon, see p. 71.)

is burried the great financier, Lawvi or Levi (p. 48)
John Law died in poverty in Venice in 1729, having been one of Europe's chief financial operators. He was a Scot (hence 'burried'), but Pound also tries to make of him another Jew of Venice, and surely sees significance in his burial place, the church of San Moisé (see next extract). Law and his death as a poor man are recalled in cantos 100 and 114, possibly in a more positive light (Law is another 'man of no fortune'). A longhand note calls for insertion of the Morosini quotation referred to in the text. Pound goes on to sketch a portrait of a Venetian contemporary of John Law, Antonio Vivaldi, in the revival of whose music he and Olga Rudge were much involved at this time. Vivaldi, known as 'the red priest', was like Pound a redhead and an organizer of musical events, and equally given to irregular affairs with at least one of his musical protégées. Pound is thinking here of his own efforts and difficulties in organizing the Rapallo concerts of the 1930s. He holds Vivaldi's music in high esteem (it was 'barely improved on' by Bach). The Latin phrase is one of Pound's slogans, and his program for *The Cantos* and poetry in general: that it should teach, move, and delight. Edouard Daladier was French prime minister in the mid-1930s; he was an unwilling signatory of the Munich agreement with Chamberlain, Hitler, and Mussolini in September 1938, by which time the final version of canto 51 had been published in *The Fifth Decad of Cantos* [42–51] (Faber, June 1937).

while they were discussing the former possibility (p. 49)
A more extended treatment of the career of John Law and of the ugly Venetian church in which he is appropriately buried. Pound sees this as confirmation that the tolerance of usury is reflected in bloated art work, like San Moisé's over-ornate façade. The typescript includes a diagram of Law's oblong tombstone and quotations from the inscription ('HONORI ET MEMORIAE / JOANNIS LAW EDINBUR-GENSIS / REGII GALLIARUM AERARII / PRAEFECTI CLARISSIMI . .

. GENTILIS SUI CINERES . . .'); 'sui generis' may be a misreading of 'gentilis'. William Hope 'Coin' Harvey (1851–1936) was an American politician and a champion of bimetallism and silver money. An English translation of Antoine Destutt de Tracy's *Treatise on Political Economy* was issued by Thomas Jefferson. Destutt's economic thought recurs in 71/420 and 87/592 ('Pity to stamp save by weight').

Lost sense of partaggio, of sharing, for fellowship (p. 51)
On the decadence of Venice, the taxes, the papacy extorting money to maintain its luxurious life style. In *Inferno* 3.18 Virgil announces that he and Dante are about to visit 'the wretched people, who have lost the good of the intellect' (*il ben dell'intelletto*), i.e., God; but Pound takes the phrase in a more general sense ('Cythera and Apollo', i.e. Venus-love and Apollo-light or creativity). The clear design of Botticelli (whose *La calunnia* is mentioned in canto 45) and Giovanni Bellini is contrasted with Titian's fleshiness. The date of the Sack of Rome, 1527, is elsewhere proposed by Pound as the turning point between the early Renaissance and decadence. The penultimate line may be read as a sort of motto: 'the phallus [is] the light of the mind' – a rather dangerous claim.

In their pageantry and their pride they were 40 (p. 53)
The anecdote is representative of Pound's notion of Mussolini as a populist concerned with economics and not with shallow ceremony.

Das endlich eine wirkliche Verständigung (p. 54)
Another typescript draft of the beginning of a canto 'XLV' (later 51). Pound was impressed by a speech given by Rudolf Hess in Königsberg in July 1934 ('It is high time that a true understanding among peoples be reached'), and quotes it in abbreviated form in canto 51 (where 'eine wirkliche Verständigung' is rendered as 'a modus vivendi'). This is a more extensive version of the association (or 'ideogram') of politics and clear-sightedness, contemplation, medieval speculation, etc., that appears, much condensed, in 51/251 (where Hess's name is omitted). As in canto 51, Pound counterpoints his attempt to define his positive and negative states ('the light of the doer' vs. usury) with excerpts from Charles Bowlker's *The Art of Angling* (1829), a document of craft and precision. Thus the poet-angler hopes to catch the fishy monster Geryon.

Work is not a commodity. No one can eat it (p. 55)
From the typescript drafts for canto 51, which also include a further page of hammering repetitions of these and similar statements (see Hesse, *Usura-Cantos*, pp. 38–39). Pound discarded these phrases in the final compacted version, which could be diagrammed as follows: Guinizelli ('Shines'), Napoleon's mud, repeat of the usura jeremiad of canto 45, the angler's art, light, intellect, Hess's modus vivendi among nations, Geryon.

III. VOICES OF WAR 1940–45

This section opens with notes Pound made for the naturalistic and mythic paradise he intended to write after completing the Chinese and American history *Cantos LII–LXXI* (1940). However, events were to lead poet and poem in a very different direction.

1940 (p. 59)
This fragment appears in Ezra Pound, *Lettere dalla Sicilia e due frammenti ritrovati* (Catania: Il Girasole, 1997). It is dated 10 June 1940, the day Italy declared war on France and England. It is 6:30 p.m., but Pound notes that (because of daylight saving time) it is really 5:30. The setting is Sant'Ambrogio di Zoagli, the hamlet above Rapallo where Olga Rudge lived. Pound notes the abundance of olive blossoms and listens to the evening church bells and to Olga playing – apparently – the fiddle part of Mozart's Sonata No. 5 for violin and piano, which she had performed with Gerhart Münch in the Rapallo concerts. Nature and culture seem to applaud the turn of events.

as against the sound of the olive mill (p. 60)
This and the following fragments evoke moments of quasi-religious immersion in nature; Greek myths appear to revive in the landscape of Liguria. References to Persephone and Tiresias are repeats of the 'fertility cantos' 39 and 47.

But here in Tigullio (p. 61)
Typescript with longhand corrections. There are some further scribbles below the last typescript line ('then stink in the sunlight'), which

is crossed out. They seem to read: 'Sap film lay (?) below (?) emerald / the sea / that then lie to stink / on the fore shore'. The harvesting of olives with bamboo poles is also described in the fine fragment 'Now sun rises in Ram sign' (*Cantos*, p. 820). The nautilus cast ashore returns (with the emerald) in a resonant elegiac passage of the Pisan cantos (80/520). Pound's 'nautile' are actually *Velella velella* (aka 'little sail', 'by the wind sailor', and in Italy as 'barchette di San Pietro', little boats of St Peter), which are quite common 'here in Tigullio' (i.e., the Gulf of Rapallo), and when cast ashore in heaps produce a strong iodine smell. The nautilus theme returns indirectly in 106/775.

as at Aquila with a hundred heads round the fountain (p. 62)
A memory of a visit to the Abruzzi. In cantos 103, 104, 105, 106 Pound was to try to recall where he had seen the landmark fountain of L'Aquila ('Fontana delle 90 cannelle') and placed it tentatively in Ovid's Sulmona. (*Bucato* is Italian for 'washing'.) The quotations from Homer refer to Eumaeus the swineherd, 'who cared more for Odysseus's possessions than all of Odysseus's slaves' (*Odyssey* 14.3–4) and to Ithaca's ancient sacred fount (17.206, 210–11), which Odysseus and Eumaeus pass on their way to the palace. (In Homer the surrounding trees are poplars, not elms as in Pound's notes.)

Washed in the Kiang & Han river (p. 63)
The opening lines are written in longhand at the end of several pages of poetic versions of Confucian texts. According to Mencius (3.1.4.13), Tsang, a disciple of Confucius, refused to render the same honours to another sage, saying: 'What has been washed in the waters of the Chiang and Han, and bleached in the autumn sun: – how glistening is it! Nothing can be added to it' (Legge, *The Works of Mencius*, p. 255). Pound transcribes the character 皓 *hào* ('spotless'), which is repeated also in the Chinese original. Tsang's metaphoric affirmation of faith-keeping returns in more ample and plangent form at the beginning of the Pisan cantos (74/445), where Pound goes on to paraphrase Mencius's next paragraph: 'Now here is this shrike-tongued barbarian of the south, whose doctrines are not those of the ancient kings' (14, cf. 74/446). The Mencius quotation recurs at the beginning of the second excerpt, which is on a separate page. (I indicate the caesura between the two passages by ellipses . . .) The latter fragment comprises five typewritten lines followed by six scribbled lines ('cloud like a sea

home' is a conjectural reading). The distinction between *techne* and *episteme* is from Aristotle, see Pound's comments on the *Nichomachean Ethics*, Book VI, in *Guide to Kulchur* (New Directions, 1952), p. 327. This is apparently not the source of the other Greek quotation ('mind over appetite'). 'what precedes and what follows' is from *The Great Learning* 3. The quoted Chinese means, 'to know what is first and what is last' (cf. 77/485, where the phrase and Chinese text recur). The character 旦 (*tan* or *dàn*, 'dawn') and the related question (from *Odes* 124) recur with esoteric implications in 97/697 and 699. The 仁 character (*rén*, benevolence) is glossed by Pound as 'humanitas'. The baking of figs is one of the local Ligurian customs he is interested in. He may be aware that *fico*, 'fig' in Italian, is vulgarly associated with the vagina (*fica*). Elsewhere he suggest that 仁 is a graph of an erection.

To attract the spirits by the beauty of jade (p. 64)
Seven typewritten lines followed by longhand notes ('at ten learn by heart the Ta Hsio...'). 'Ta Hsio' (pinyin *Dà xuê*) is *The Great Learning*, twice translated by Pound (and cited in previous fragment: 'what precedes and what follows').

saying: O Kat based upon reason (p. 65)
Lines 1–2 are added in longhand to the typescript, as are the last five lines. 'Kat' may allude to Pound's beloved cats, but this is far from certain (it could be short for 'category'). The fragment contains further paraphrases of Confucian Ode 124 ('White the pillow of horn', see above). The references to Latin myth and ritual can be compared with cantos 39, 47, and the lynx canto (79/507–12). Pound admired and often quoted the *Pervigilium Veneris*. Cleopatra's familiarity with economics is mentioned again in canto 85. Theodora is presumably Justinian's empress (91/631), another 'belle dame sans merci' (and sans pudeur).

for which the wind is quiet (p. 66)
A page of manuscript and typescript notes, with three versions of the same passage about fire and beauty, of which I print the second and third, both typewritten; the equation of mind and love ('nous – amor') I take from the first handwritten draft. 'Freedom not privilege' recalls a dictum by Mussolini often quoted by Pound: 'Freedom is not a right

but a duty' (cf. 78/499). At the bottom, *shi ming ming* is intended as an equivalent of 'to spread this effulgence'.

With a white flash of wings over the dawn light (p. 67)
Pound continues to mine the Confucian scriptures for phrases, wisdom and reassurance. We know that he pocketed Legge's bilingual *Four Books* when he was arrested in May 1945, and some of these phrases recur in the Pisan cantos. Confucius's summation of the import of the *Odes*, 'Have no twisty thoughts' (*Analects* 2.2), appears in Chinese at the end of Pound's translation of the *Odes*. It could possibly be read as a motto for *The Cantos*, which are also a compilation and 'Book of Odes'.

The holiness of the lord has a blister (p. 68)
Manuscript. This looks like a dirge for Mussolini's fall from power (July 23, 1943). 'ex-XXI', is 1943, the twenty-first year of the defunct Fascist Era. Pound cites the opening lines of his well-known early poem 'Ballatetta', from *Canzoni* (1911), and proceeds with his anthropological notations. Mussolini may have gone, but *The Cantos* remain to be written. '[...]' indicates undeciphered words.

So that in August, of the year ex-XXI (p. 69)
A parallel between the fall of Mussolini in July 1943 and Napoleon's Hundred Days, with material taken from the *Gazzetta di Genova* for 1815. Pound borrowed the latter from his acquaintance Massimo Ruggero Bacigalupo, the Rapallo pharmacist (who owned a run of the old *Gazzetta* and was probably showing friends the 1815 bound volume to comment on the sudden removal by state edict of twenty years' worth of Fascist insignia). Pound's notes may have been written after September 12, 1943, when Mussolini was rescued by German paratroopers and, like Napoleon in 1815, engineered a comeback, though aware by this point that he was but Hitler's pawn. Mussolini's forced resurrection and the consequent establishment of the puppet 'Social Republic' of Salò (RSI) inaugurated the civil war that raged in northern Italy until April 1945. Boris III of Bulgaria died August 28, 1943, aged forty-seven, probably poisoned on Hitler's orders for opposing the deportation of Jews from his kingdom and in general holding his own against his German ally, but Pound probably thought that Boris was another popular leader removed by a bankers'

conspiracy. From the 1815 *Gazzetta* Pound extracts details of the aristocratic pageants at the Congress of Vienna, to suggest the frivolousness of Napoleon's opponents. He then attempts to correlate the *Gazzetta*'s financial reports with Napoleon's alternating fortunes and final defeat at Waterloo. Bonaparte is presented as a popular leader, welcomed by the people and hated by the old regime. At the end of his notes from the *Gazzetta di Genova*, Pound marked the dates of Napoleon's departure from Elba and of Waterloo. On a separate page he made further longhand notes on funds and bonds and drafted the lines, 'after which for 100 years . . . usury', which he then typed and extended on another leaf. Here he introduces a memory of what was said in his presence about how long it would take to get rid of Mussolini as had been done with Napoleon (a scene recorded with further details in 78/497, as well as in *Carta da visita*, see *Selected Prose 1909–1965*, Faber 1973, p. 313). Again, the suggestion is that the populist hero is a disturbance to the status quo that must be maintained at all cost. 'name, address' is another oft-repeated Mussolini saying about personal accountability (versus the anonymous conspirators): 'wherein is no responsible person / having a front name, a hind name and an address' (78/499). The two last lines are added in longhand.

The cat stars have shut one eye (p. 73)
A MS fragment concerning Pound's short visit to Gais, South Tyrol, after his adventurous departure from Rome after the Armistice between Italy and the Allies, September 8, 1943. He quotes a German language newspaper that denounces Italy's sudden exit from the alliance with Germany. A German voice complains: 'You can present this as a necessity but you will never find an excuse for the fact that this happened without at least warning the allied powers [i.e, Germany]'. Actually, the Germans were expecting this turn of events since the fall of Mussolini in July 1943, and immediately occupied northern Italy. Margherita, a Gais figure, is mentioned in 77/491 – Pound had good memory.

Ub. – (p. 74)
These are longhand notes on Pound's trip from Rome to Gais, where he joined his much-loved eighteen-year-old daughter Mary. 'Ub' is his friend Ubaldo degli Uberti (77/493, 93/648, 95/664). Pound

passed along the Via Salaria through Settebagni ('7 Bagni'), a Rome suburb, on his way to Fara Sabina and Rieti. 'Vinum generosum' (Latin) is 'hearty wine'. There is a medieval song, 'istu vinum bonum vinum vinum generosu[m]'. Wine ('vino') is mentioned three times in this memorandum (the distracted wanderer may have needed it to fortify himself), as well as 'uova' (eggs) and 'uva' (grapes). These notes should be compared with the expanded account of Pound's journey in 78/498, where some of the phrases are translated: 'Nothing left but women', 'nothing to pay for that bread / nor for the minestra'. Pound had an ear for phrases and he was clearly in a state of heightened emotion during this solitary trip in the midst of private and public chaos. He also used it as a starting point for the pamphlet *Oro e lavoro*: 'On the 10th September last, I walked down the Via Salaria and into the Republic of Utopia, a quiet country lying eighty years east of Fara Sabina' (*Selected Prose 1909–1965*, p. 336).

Maderno, and there was calm in the stillness (p. 75)
Published as 'Fragment, 1944' by Christine Froula in *Yale Review* 71.2 (1982), pp. 161–64. Memories of a visit in November 1943 to the Lake Garda headquarters of the Salò Republic, and quotations from Confucian scriptures, frame a further series of flashes of Pound's September journey from 'fallen' Rome to the Tyrol, when he heard the 'catlike' cries of the *barbagianni* (barn owls). The 'Alban' hills are south of Rome, so perhaps he uses the name here in a generic sense (*alba* as 'dawn'). Again, some of the phrases Pound caught are recovered in 78/498 ('Who *says* he is an American'). The link between Garda (Benacus), where Pound met the 'prefect' Gioacchino Nicoletti, and Pound's solo journey, is provided by the 'stillness outlasting all wars' (74/447). He is leaving behind his wartime fury and entering a more contemplative condition. Again he quotes from the esoteric Confucian Ode 124. The 'stillness' is emphasized in the account of the encounter with Nicoletti in canto 74, where the prefect exclaims: 'La donna, la donna…'. ('Woman!' – enough said.) Pound is regaining his composure. Gioacchino Nicoletti (Rieti 1897–Perugia 1983) was a personal collaborator of Mussolini, albeit a moderate, as well as a scholar. Maderno is a town near Salò. Canto 74 repeats the observation that a mountain on Lake Garda reminds Pound of Mount Fuji in Japan, just as China's Mt Taishan is said to loom over the Pisa detention centre: 'from the death cells in sight of Mt Taishan @ Pisa

/ as Fujiyama at Gardone, / when the cat walked the top bar of the railing' (74/447). The final Confucian sayings appear again in 77/488.

360 thousand and sorrow, sorrow like rain (p. 77)
Typescript with longhand corrections and additions. These are images from Mussolini's aggression towards Greece, and of Germany's intervention in aid of the Italians (1941). 'Possum' is Pound's usual nickname for T. S. Eliot, cf. 74/445. Eliot's friend Jean Verdenal had been killed in WW1 at Gallipoli, where the Australian and New Zealand Army Corps (ANZAC) suffered heavy losses in 1915, and this is probably the reason of Eliot's appearance here. The Greek words mean 'immortal way, immortal song'.

So that he put up a saw mill, and they took him (p. 78)
A first-hand account of the underequipped and unprepared Italian army, of the endless succession of wars abroad, and of corruption at home. Pound's source, whose name seems to be Filippo di Stefano, concludes on a positive note: 'In sum, humanity isn't vile'. Italy invaded Albania in April 1939; Genoa was bombed by the British navy in February 1941.

m'apparve in quel triedro (p. 79)
Bilingual draft concerning the meeting with a ghostly woman near Pound and Olga's house in Sant'Ambrogio, in a place that he calls 'il triedro', possibly a personal variant for 'trivium'. Translation: 'She appeared to me in that trihedron: "I am the moon"'. A *mulattiera* is a mule-path. Pound imagines a procession of ghosts: the arcane moon-lady, Sigismondo Malatesta, Lorenzo de' Medici, Confucius, Buddha, Scotus Erigena... He guesses that the lady may be Cunizza da Romano, an important figure in Dante's *Paradiso* as well as in *The Cantos* (6/22, 29/142, etc.), where she is associated with her lover the poet Sordello (see 'Three Cantos' I). The numinous 'triedro' and the wraiths Pound encounters there are a leitmotif of the Pisan cantos ('E al Triedro, Cunizza / e l'altra [and the other woman]: "Io son la Luna"' – 74/458). 'Sigismundo' (Pound's preferred spelling) appears against the same background ('by the Aurelia to Genova') in 76/472. The image of the 'great periplum' Pound uses at the beginning of the Pisan cantos. 'Wan' is probably Wen Wang, one of the great emperors

(53/265, etc.), see also 'Decade of King Wen' (*Confucian Odes* 235–244). This draft appears to be a synthesis of recurrent motifs.

ERIGENA (p. 80)
The great Irish Neo-Platonist thinker Johannes Scotus Erigena expatiates in a stage-Irish brogue on Dante and other matters, referring in particular to Dante's explanatory letter to Cangrande della Scala, 'the big dog' (Pound's 'big BowWow'). This passage is among the extensive drafts Pound wrote chiefly in Italian in 1944–45; it is included here because it is partly in English. I have omitted about thirty lines in Italian (indicated by '. . .'), variants of which can be found in the next section. The quotations from Antoninus Pius, 'Cheu' (Zhu Ying, a member of the Chinese legation in Rome and a friend of sinologist Fengchi Tang, aka Lionello Lanciotti) and Brancusi, recur in the post-war cantos: '"These people" said Mr Tcheou "should / be like brothers. They read the same books" / meaning chinese and japanese' (88/602); 'And Brancusi repeating: je peux commencer / une chose tous les jours, mais / finiiiir' (86/580, also 97/697). See below, *aint no son of a bitch can help me.*

V. ITALIAN DRAFTS 1944–1945

After the Italian cantos 72–73 (1944–45), Pound produced extensive drafts for further Italian cantos (winter-spring 1944–45), which never reached final form. When he began writing the Pisan sequence in summer 1945, this recent work was in his mind and he made ample use of images and phrases from the Italian drafts in some of the most haunting pages of the new sequence. I offer here an edited text of significant passages, with my English translation. I have regularized somewhat Pound's erratic Italian spelling and syntax, and replaced the slashes (/), much used in the typescript, with conventional punctuation. In my English translation standard forms of proper names are used. Many of these drafts have been published, translated, and annotated by Ron Bush, see for example *A Poem Including History*, ed. Lawrence Rainey (University of Michigan Press, 1996), pp. 169–212; *Modernism and the Orient*, ed. Zhaoming Qian (UNO Press, 2012), pp. 185–200.

Accade ogni mezzo secolo una meraviglia (pp. 84/85)
[*Every half century a marvel occurs*]
Pound recalls an occasion in Rome, 'perhaps in the ninth year' (of the Fascist calendar, i.e., 1931), in which he became tipsy and had a vision of the return of the gods and of the eternal cycles of war and peace. In a 1945 interview in Washington with psychiatrist Jerome Kavka, he recollected 'a few historic drunks, one when . . . I prophesied the return of the Pagan Gods about ten years ago' – *Paideuma* 20.1–2 (1991), p. 157. This may be the occasion recorded here, and again in the Pisan cantos: 'and from under the Rupe Tarpeia / drunk with wine of the Castelli / "in the name of its god"' (74/463). 'La Rupe Tarpea' was a restaurant in Via Veneto, Rome, named after the Capitol's Tarpeian Rock (from which misbegotten Roman newborns were hurled to their death – mentioned also in 117/821). Inebriated by the sparkling wine of the Albergo Pace (near the Trajan Column, not far from the Capitol), Pound remembers Rimbaud's 'Au Cabaret-Vert', a poem he translated, and his old flame Iseult Gonne, with whom he remained in amicable correspondence until her death in 1954 (104/761). He is carried away by a sense of the eternal return ('akasa' is the 'astral plane' in yoga and perhaps the cycle of eternal recurrence, cf. the 44,000 years in *By the arena*, above). In *Carta da visita* (1942) Pound envisages 'replacing the marble goddess on her pedestal at Terracina', a village on the Circeo promontory (*Selected Prose 1909–1965*, p. 320). In the last lines the eternal goddess takes on the domestic features of a remembered woman. Her Greek epithets recur at the end of the Pisan lynx canto (79/512).

Ripresero allora i dolci suoni (pp. 88/89)
[*Then began again the sweet sounds*]
This is the scene that the Italian drafts often revert to, as do the Pisan cantos: the meeting with ghostly ladies among the olive trees, on the Sant'Ambrogio hillside. The Provençal quotation is the opening line of a poem on birdsong by Arnaut Daniel. Galla Placidia appears in the Italian canto 72/430, where in fact her conversation with Pound is 'interrupted' by the furious ghost of Ezzelino da Romano clamouring for revenge. The suggestion of a carnival company returns in the vision of 81/540.

In un triedro dell'oliveto mi apparve (pp. 90/91)

[*In a triedro of the olive grove she appeared to me*]

This long draft (four typescript pages) was arranged by Pound as a tentative 'canto 74'. (I use inverted commas to distinguish these discarded Italian canto-drafts from cantos 74–75 as published.) I have reordered the material somewhat and inserted a few passages from other versions of the same episodes; lines 1–5 are from an earlier manuscript, dated '12 febbraio' (probably 1945). The poet converses with several spirits: Cunizza da Romano (who speaks of her savage yet loyal brother Ezzelino, chief presence of canto 72) and the poet Basinio of Rimini, both familiar to readers of *The Cantos*, and Caterina (Riario) Sforza, ruler of Imola and in 1488 dauntless defender of Forlì against Cesare Borgia: according to an old story, when her enemies threatened to kill her sons, she 'raised her skirt' to show her pubes, saying: 'I still have the mould' (76/472). The first Provençal quotation ('Negus vezer') is not from Sordello (as would appear from the context) but from Bernart de Ventadorn ('Can par la flors josta.l vert folh', cf. 20/89, 92/639). The apparition of Sigismondo Malatesta on his way to Genoa recurs in canto 76, as well as the mention of San Pantaleo, a small church on the so-called 'Roman' Aurelia near 'Casa 60', Pound's home in Sant'Ambrogio. The etymological pun on 'Pantaleone', which suggests that the saint's name incorporates ancient solar rituals ('helion'), is taken from another draft concerning Malatesta; I have inserted it here because indicative of Pound's mythical reading of his chosen landscapes. The chapel of San Pantaleo appears also in the 1942 fragment 'Now sun rises in Ram sign' (*Cantos*, p. 820). For Arnaut's 'Doutz brais e criz', see above, *Ripresero allora i dolci suoni*; 'traiz pena' ('suffered pain') is from Ventadorn's 'Tant ai mo cor ple de joya'. The closing phrases Pound lifted from a Latin poem by Johannes Scotus Erigena, praising Ermentrude of Orléans, wife of Charles the Bald: 'perfect in Pallas's art, prepares silk threads with thin gold . . . the cloaks of her spouse' (cf. 83/548 and *Patrologia Latina* 122.1227).

14 Jan (pp. 98/99)

[*14 Jan*]

Typescript draft of a provisional 'canto 75', pp. 1–4 (of 6). I have omitted passages that are variants of other drafts. On p. 4 there is a brief repeat of the apparition of Buddha and Confucius from the end of the previous draft ('canto 74', p. 3). I have replaced this with a somewhat different version of the same vision from another type-script, which refers also to Kuan Yin or Kwannon, Chinese goddess of mercy. The opening image of the sun conducting his fleet of stars, planets and nymphs 'under our craggy cliffs' (76/472) was to recur (in English) at the beginning of the Pisan cantos (74/445), most extensively in 76/472. In canto 23 we are told that Anchises, father of Aeneas, heard island women 'howling because Adonis died virgin' (23/109). Pound goes on to images of war, reverts to Erigena's discussion of Dante (see above, 'Voices of War'), and to Queen Ermentrude's weaving her royal husband's shirts. (For 'al fuso ed al pennecchio' ['at the spindle and the flax'] see Dante, *Paradiso* 15.117 – the description of ancient and virtuous Florence.) Other ghostly presences are Malatesta, his court poet Basinio, Cosimo de' Medici (whose role as peace-maker in Naples is mentioned in canto 21, which also refers to Diotisalvi Nerone), Lorenzo de' Medici and Savonarola. 'Saja' and 'rascia' are archaic terms for two kinds of fine cloth, sometimes mentioned together. Detailed annotations for these Italian 'cantos' 74–75 can be found in *Paideuma* 20.1–2 (1991), pp. 30–40.

Dove la salita scende e fa triedro (pp. 106/107)
[*Where the path descends and makes a triedro*]
This is another version of the poet's meeting in the rural Ligurian landscape with a mysterious girl, here described as *scalza* (barefoot). She says that she has fled from the 'ruined' church of the Madonna delle Grazie (near Chiavari, a few miles south of Rapallo), to seek refuge in the chapel of San Pantaleo. Cf. 76/473: 'La scalza: Io son la luna / and they have broken my house'. Pound may be alluding also to the damage done to the main Rapallo church by Allied aircraft, July 28, 1944. In the tragic last years of the war it was common to encounter on the road vagabonds and homeless people in varying states of dejection and confusion.

Mai con codardi (codini) sarà l'arte monda (p.p 108/109)
[*Never with cowards (fogies) will art be mended*]
This notable passage belongs to the draft of the Italian 'canto 75' (pp. 4–5). The speaker is the Goddess, identified with the Christian Virgin, who has escaped from her ruined shrines. Another typescript version of this passage has been preserved, and is titled 'ASSUNTA (?dopo Cunizza) dopo ascesa', i.e. 'the Virgin of the Assumption (?after

Cunizza) after the ascent'. From this version I have taken the arrangement of the line about the 'fano delle Grazie' (the shrine of Nostra Signora delle Grazie above Chiavari mentioned in the previous fragment). This quasi-religious incantation was first drafted in the same manuscript notebook in which Pound composed the Italian cantos 72–73, and is dated 12 January (1945). In this first draft Pound wrote 'sotto le vaghe stelle dell'Orso' (under the beauteous stars of the Great Bear), misquoting the first line of Giacomo Leopardi's 'Le ricordanze' ('Vaghe stelle dell'Orsa, io non credea...'); in the typescript versions 'vaghe' disappears perhaps because not easy to decipher, and so the pointed allusion to Leopardi is lost. The scene with the 'pargoletto' ('little boy', like the child Jesus in images of the Virgin) recurs (also in Italian) in 80/520. Salmasius (Claude Saumaise, John Milton's adversary) was the author of *De Modo Usurarum*, one of Pound's canonical texts.

Ogni beato porta con sé il cielo (pp. 112/113)
[*Every blessed soul carries along with it the heavenly sphere*]
Draft of 'canto 75', pp. 5–6. The Dantesque notion of the blessed carrying with them their particular heavenly sphere returns in drafts for canto 81, see below, *Ed ascoltando al leggier mormorio*.

Nel periplo che fa il vostro Sole (pp. 116/117)
[*In the periplum that your Sun makes*]
'Canto 75', p. 6. A reprise of the image of the Sun as admiral leading his fleet to the cliffs in time of war. Among Pound's many eccentric spellings, 'scoglie' for 'scogli' (rocks, cliffs) recurs in the original printings of canto 76: 'sotto le nostre scoglie' (cf. 76/472); Pound wrote his daughter that he wanted this corrected to 'scogli' (*Paideuma* 37 (2010), p. 200), so the lines should read: 'sotto i nostri scogli / under our craggy cliffs'

e i fiocchi giaccion e fondon (pp. 118/119)
[*and the snowflakes lie and melt*]
This page, a continuation of the previous fragment, is the last of four leaves Pound titled 'Eliseo' (possibly meaning 'Elysium', i.e., Heaven). We are still listening to the voices of the daughters of the sun, describing a sort of earthly paradise. Vail de Lencour is the pseudonym used by Pound for Brigit Patmore in the dedication of *Lustra*;

Jean Verdenal is the dedicatee of *Prufrock and Other Observations*, so the 'friend' he is waiting for in his earthly paradise is T. S. Eliot. The author of *The Death of Felicity Taverner* (1932) was Mary Butts, who died in 1937. Aliscamps is the Roman burial place in Arles, recalled by Dante in *Inferno* 9 and by Pound in 80/532. The Sirens tell Ulysses 'We know all the toils that in wide Troy the Argives and Trojans endured', a phrase from *Odyssey* 12 quoted in Greek in Pound's *Mauberley* and alluded to in 6/21.

Come è ch'io sento le vetuste voci (pp. 120/121)
[*How is it that I hear the ancient voices*]
The opening question heads one of the typescript pages titled 'Eliseo', where it is followed by a variant of *In the periplum that your Sun makes* (above). The following more speculative description of the Confucian-Taoist 'process' occupies another full page of the 'Eliseo' sequence.

Se in febbraio il freddo rilascia la morsa (pp. 124/125)
[*If in February the cold relaxes its bite*]
A self-standing typescript fragment, with quotations from *Pervigilium Veneris* (alluded to also in canto 79). On this leaf Pound noted in longhand a tentative ordering of the materials he had composed in Italian: 'Salita / Cunizza / shift / Basinio / Sidg. [Malatesta] / La Rocca [The Fortress] / uscita [exit] / Imp. [Roman Emperors] / Asunta / Cat. Sforza / Erigena / Eliseo'. So 'Eliseo' with the image of the venerated goddess of many names and religions would have been the climax of the Italian sequence, had it been completed.

VI. PISA 1945

a quando? (p. 129)
From the Pisa notebooks, pp. 87–94, late July 1945. Pound was brought to the US Army Disciplinary Center, north of Pisa, on May 24, and began making notes for cantos in July. This omitted passage occurs in the manuscript that became the first long Pisan canto, between the lines 'rain, Ussel' and 'To the left of la bella Torre' (74/456). I have used the transcript published by Ron Bush in *Paideuma* 32.1–2–3 (2003), pp. 181–86, with additions and corrections provided for this edition by Bush. For the sake of clarity of presentation, I have made a

few changes to spelling and lineation. Much of the material appears later in the Pisan cantos, and can be identified and glossed by readers familiar with the published poem. However, the memories of 'Possum' Eliot in the Dordogne caverns (i.e., Les Eyzies) and the affectionate eulogy of 'fat' Ford Madox Ford do not occur in the printed text. Nor does the significant quotation from W. S. Blunt, which anticipates the climactic statement at the close of canto 81 (again in connection with Blunt): 'But to have done instead of not doing . . .'. Pound also reverts to his 1943 journey from Rome to the Tyrol (see above, *Maderno*, etc.) and to the theme of the 'betrayed' Mussolini (compared to Manes). 'Edda' (Ciano) is the Duce's mercurial and unrepentant daughter, who is reported as saying that her father could have expected treason everywhere, 'but not in the King's house' (cf. 103/753). It was in fact Victor Emmanuel III who had Mussolini arrested at Villa Savoia on July 24, 1943. But, as Pound points out here and elsewhere (80/516), the Duce's enemies mistakenly believed that they could 'buy' the house (Italy) from the janitor (the king), who could not deliver the goods – for the German army took control of northern Italy in September 1943. Pound continues to proclaim Mussolini's essential honesty and to portray him as a populist. In an earlier omitted passage from the notebook (p. 76), he writes: 'murdered for his good will – not for his vices / the privileged did not / like social improvements / or wage regulations'. 'a quando' means 'till when?', a form of goodbye. In the opening lines, 'aspetto la diana' (I am waiting for the clarion call [of resurgence]) is from 73/438. Perigueux recalls the Aliscamps at Arles and Dante's allusion to them, see above, *e i fiocchi giaccion e fondon*. Two further lines adapted from Dante occur towards the end, see *Inferno* 1.26 ('I turned back to see the pass') and *Paradiso* 5.105 ('who will increase our loves'). The final sentence in Italian is Pound's own statement: 'I went to Paradise and passed this plain'. The Chinese phrases in the margin mostly correspond to Pound's English quotations from the Four Books ('when not of man, is of heaven', 'two parts of a tally stick', 'private gain is not prosperity'). These freewheeling notes, with their mention of labyrinths, coherence, reality, and the impossibility of bringing salvation (perhaps to his daughter), convey a striking impression of a mind seeking its bearings in confusion.

Ed ascoltando al leggier mormorio (p. 134)
This is the ghostly visitation of canto 81 as first drafted in Pound's

notebook (pp. 247–51). The lines in brackets are crossed out. Pound compacted the draft when preparing his typescript (omitting line 2, among others) and made further cuts in the New Directions proofs (now at Butler Library, Columbia University). He cancelled the Dantesque reflection on the souls moving through each other but keeping their outline (a variation of the Italian draft *Ogni beato porta con sé il cielo*, above), as well as the pentameter couplet describing Althea's ghostly kiss. The latter explains more fully what he meant by the 'palpable elysium', preserved in the published text – nothing less than a kiss. '*eidos*' (εἶδος, printed as Eidὼς at 81/540) is 'form', 'beauty', 'quality', 'nature'. Opposite notebook page 250 Pound noted an alternative version of his quasi-philosophical musing: '[nor was there space] for the full *eidos* of the form / to pass & intercross. / each space full of its formal life / that moves and keeps defined / its clarity, demarcations. / what thou lovest well, / remains, / the rest is dross'. This is one of the few passages of the Pisan cantos that Pound revised extensively; in the final redaction he preserved the essence of his notes emphasizing their suggestiveness and visionary vagueness. The subject is the apparition in the prisoner's Pisan tent of loving (female) eyes and masks, a fantasy of light and visual music, which leads him to the comforting 'certainty' that beauty and love endure among chaos. ('carneval', retained in the final version, is the Italian spelling of 'carnival'.)

Yet from my tomb such flame of love arise (p. 136)
This valediction originally opened canto 84, last of the Pisan sequence. Cats and the search for private and public peace are recurrent themes. The lines were omitted from the published text possibly because they were too traditional and elegiac in form, and because Pound had as yet no intention of composing an epitaph for himself à la Yeats. Thus canto 84 as we have it opens more robustly with a multilingual epitaph not for Pound but for his poet friend and R. A. F. pilot J. P. Angold (84/557).

Night rain and a Biddle sky (p. 137)
This long passage occurred at the end of canto 84, above the current final couplet about the hoarfrost (84/560). Pound cancelled all of it, preserving only the couplet, which serves as an effective close to the Pisan cantos. The result of this drastic cut is to make canto 84 much

shorter and less digressive. The text presented here is based on Pound's typescript, with some corrections and additions (e.g., the Chinese) from the notebook version. Pound mentions his sixtieth birthday (October 30, 1945) and continues to write in early November. Nicholas Biddle was president of the Second Bank of the United States and an adversary of Andrew Jackson, one of Pound's heroes. Francis Biddle was US Attorney General at the time of Pound's indictment. Thus 'a Biddle sky' must be a lowering sky. 'Ascreus' is an epithet of Hesiod, father of Greek poetry, see *Homage to Sextus Propertius* 12. Once again Pound recounts with further details his escape from Rome in September 1943 (see above, *Maderno, Ub –,* and *a quando?*) as the beginning of a 'new life' (the allusion is to the opening of Dante's *Vita nuova*). He reverts to the iniquity of gun sales and FDR, considers the landscape and the insect life in the camp's grass, and reports that it is more difficult to keep the peace between two litigious concubines than to govern an empire, obviously thinking of his wife Dorothy and his companion Olga, who in 1944–45 lived by necessity under one roof. He also reports a trenchant comment of Olga on self-destructive Italian factionalism, and her name appears in its entirety (another reason perhaps for the omission of these pages). Pound continues to reflect on the cost of war and suggests that WW2 could have been avoided (Joseph Davies was US ambassador to Moscow, 1937–38). As usual, he presents himself as a master of the intricacies of world politics and as the confidant of statesmen. He quotes the hymn 'God the Omnipotent!' (also known as 'Russian Hymn') and notes that the alleged Russian original should be inserted here – never missing an opportunity to include another language in the poem. (He also wanted to approach Stalin, referred to favourably here as well as in 84/560.) He continues with the couplet preserved in the final version (autumn cold has come to Pisa) and with a rhapsodic invocation of Italy (contrasting with Olga's reported criticism of Italians). In the notebook draft (p. 308) this outburst is followed by the lines transcribed here (brackets indicate a conjectural reading). They include a quatrain of anti-psychiatric satire, with the notation that it is not meant for *The Cantos*, and a reprise of the theme of the war's young victims. Saturno Montanari (1918–41) was an unknown poet whom Pound translated. The last date in the margin is 14 November – two days before Pound's repatriation.

VII. PROSAIC VERSES 1950–1960

This section offers a selection of notes made by Pound while detained at St Elizabeths Hospital in Washington, D.C., and after his return to Italy. The title is borrowed from a booklet he published in 1959, *Versi prosaici*, containing excerpts from the same material. In a brief Italian justification for *Versi prosaici*, Pound explained: 'These Prosaic Verses do not belong to the Cantos (to Los Cantares) but perhaps they will clarify some of their refrains to the benevolent reader' (p. 59). The same can be said of the excerpts printed here.

and my gt/ aunt's third husband (p. 145)
Lines quoted in *I Cantos*, ed. Mary de Rachewiltz (Mondadori, 1985), p. 1536. Canto 49 is based on eight Chinese landscape poems in an illustrated screen book (Japanese, eighteenth century) that reached Pound through a circuitous route, as recorded here. See above the openings drafted for canto 49, especially *Spent yesterday drawing a grasshopper*. Pound's screen book is reproduced in colour in *Ezra Pound e i Sette Laghi*, ed. Maria Costanza De Luca (Diabasis, 2002). For an account of Pound's source, see *Ezra Pound and China*, ed. Zhaoming Quian (University of Michigan Press, 2003), pp. 72–95. 'Hsin ji' is, in Chinese, the motto Pound rendered as 'Make It New'. Cf. 94/662, which also aligns the ancient Chinese injunction with the Neo-Platonist Ocellus.

Ian had felt it: 'blown to pieces? (p. 146)
This passage and the ones that follow are excerpted from a typescript of forty-six pages, numbered 13–60 (pp. 20, 26 and 28 are missing), that Pound or an associate copied from his manuscript notebooks, indicating notebook number (8, 7b, 9 'Jan '51', 10, 11 'Sept 52', 12 'Ag/ 51', '4 or 13????', '14 verso', 15, 16, 17 'Oct '52'). Compare Mary de Rachewiltz, *A Catalogue of the Poetry Notebooks of Ezra Pound* (Yale University Library, 1980). It is likely that Pound had this typescript prepared so that he could borrow from it in future cantos, which is what he did to mostly brilliant effect in *Rock-Drill* (the section completed 1954), less happily in the last part of *Thrones* (cantos 100–105), possibly completed in Italy, 1958–59. The present excerpt (typescript, p. 13, given in its entirety) repeats the theme of the peace-makers, among whom Pound counts Edward VIII (as well

as himself). We then hear of writers and artists who died in WW1, 'thus changing the English language' (if this is Pound's meaning). Giovanni Boldini is cited as a salon portraitist in contrast with the genius of Brancusi (whose phrase on precious time, presumably when the artist is fully engaged in creation, appears in 85/579). For Judith Gautier, see 80/524. The Greek phrase is from Pausanias (2.34.10): 'They perform secret rights for Demeter' ('of Lycian Apollo' is Pound's addition).

'aint no son of a bitch can help me' (p. 148)
Typescript, pp. 14–15. For Tcheou and his comment see above, *ERIGENA*, 88/602, and *Carta da visita* (*Selected Prose 1909–1965*, p. 313). The Lawrence Binyon quotation recurs in an important passage, 87/592. For Humboldt and Agassiz see 89/618. The Heraclitean 'flow' (*hrein*) is cited at 107/782, 'phyllotaxis' in the lyric canto 106/774. In this period Pound was fascinated by the natural sciences and by scientists like Louis Agassiz; he listed in *The Cantos* the names of plants, and wondered about their genetic characteristics ('oak leaf never plane leaf' – 87/593).

'one god and Mahomet' stamped by Roger of Sicily (p. 149)
Typescript, p. 17. Statements of religious syncretism, and allusions to Henry James and his 'parentheses', his convoluted sentences, to justify Pound's need to digress ceaselessly.

John Heydon, the signatures (p. 150)
Typescript, p. 19 (entire). For John Heydon, see above, p. 183, and cantos 87, 91 and 92. (At St Elizabeths, Pound borrowed Yeats's copy of Heydon's *Holy Guide* from Mrs Yeats; 'signatures' are signs or ciphers in nature.) Again Pound sketches a rationale for his fragmentary style; likewise on p. 25 he notes: 'the point *is* that all this stuff hangs together. / I am not repeating H.J.'. He goes on to the economic theme of 'chreia' (demand), a term he encountered in the *Nicomachean Ethics* (cf. 87/590), and to quote Marianne Moore, a fan of the Brooklyn Dodgers. Her reference, however, seems to be to the New York Giants pitcher Christy Mathewson – not to the Harvard scholar F. O. Matthiessen. 'Sensibility' and 'curiosity' are important leitmotifs in the later cantos, see especially the beginning of canto 85.

'daily exercise or more power than any President' (p. 152)
Typescript, p. 25. Opening line marked in margin 'n/bk 9 / Jan '51'.
Notes from Pound's reading on the Jackson administration, obviously
related to the powers invested in the President. W. S. Landor did in
fact compose an 'Ode to General Jackson', who is contrasted here
with Pound's *bête noire*, FDR. The 'four tuan', or principles of Confu-
cianism, are given prominence in cantos 85 and 89. 'Juan Ramon'
could be the Spanish poet Juan Ramón Jiménez (90/627), but more
likely Pound's Catalan friend Juan Ramón Masoliver, a contributor
to the 'Literary Supplement' of the Rapallo weekly *Mare* (co-ed-
ited by Pound, 1932–33). 'Now I remember . . .' is a savage parody
of one of Pound's most haunting imitations of the Chinese, 'Exile's
Letter' (after Li Po). For 'metathemenon', another economic nugget
from Aristotle, see the close of canto 76. The character *chih* (*zhi*) is
glossed in Pound's *Confucius* as 'The will, the direction of the will,
directio voluntatis, the officer standing over the heart', cf. 77/487. In
De Vulgari Eloquentia 2.2, Dante speaks of three subjects appropriate
to (vernacular) poetry: war, love, and virtue, and glosses the latter as
'directio voluntatis', which became one of Pound's touchstones.

The EMPEROR ploughed his furrow and his wife (p. 154)
Typescript, p. 44. These notes were successfully recast in 87/592–93
and 90/625; in the latter the allusion to Mozart's *Magic Flute* is
replaced by Amphion's trumpet. The Greek words, from Sophocles's
Women of Trachis, appear also in 87/591. 'e dica cala non dica converso'
is from a Canzone to Fortune, 'Io son la donna che volgo la rota',
which Rossetti translated (attributing it doubtfully to Cavalcanti) and
Pound quoted as genuine in *The Spirit of Romance*, as well as in cantos
86, 96 and 97. Pound also set to music this canzone as a finale for his
opera *Cavalcanti*. Rossetti renders the quoted line as 'Nor say because
he fell I did him wrong'.

for a word / for the mistranslation of XREIA (p. 155)
Typescript, p. 50. For 'chreia' (demand) see above. (Pound always
transliterates the Greek letter 'chi' as 'X'.) For the trees of Count Piti-
gliano see 10/42. 'Sowbelly' is FDR. The hunchback ('gobbo') Luigi,
a pedlar in Sant'Ambrogio, appears as an exponent of natural reli-
gion in 97/699 and 106/773. The Chinese is a proverbial phrase, 'At

fifty, study is easy'. Bertran de Born, the troubadour, is one of Pound's major personae, see the long poem 'Near Périgord'.

L'arif est gai, de bonne humeur, souriant (p. 156)
Typescript, pp. 51–53 (end of Notebook 16). The passage opens with notes on good humour in connection with religion. 'Aarif' is an Arab name which is said to connote a happy person. The Chinese phrases mean 'One word can ruin a deal' and 'One man can fix a kingdom'. Pound recalls his friendly reception in 1908 in the synagogue of Gibraltar, reported at length in canto 22. He mourns dead and ailing friends of his youth like Stella Bowen and Wyndham Lewis. He remembers Mussato's account of the Satanic birth of Ezzelino da Romano, though thinking of other allegedly Satanic engenderings. These infernal doings are set against the Fascist 'ventennio' (two decades, 1922–1943), whose 'will' and 'power' appear to him intimated by a stone pulpit in Brescia. The recurring character 義 (*yì*, 'righteousness') is glossed as 'onestade' and 'bontade' (93/646–47, cf. 86/583, 97/694, 98/709). Subsequent notes refer to empress Maria Theresa of Austria, for whose enlightened policies (economic, social and cultural) Pound has nothing but admiration.

Old Peters after '48 that was (p. 159)
Typescript, pp. 55–56. Pound lists some of his many heroes: Talleyrand; Bismarck; his ancestor Joseph Wadsworth, who in 1687 hid the Connecticut Charter in an oak-tree (*Indiscretions* and cantos 97, 109 and 111); the Jesuit sinologist Prospero Intorcetta (104/762); and alludes to a bank carrying the surname of Pope Eugenio Pacelli (Pius XII). I have found this phrase (repeated in 100/739) in Joseph Schmidlin, *Papstgeschichte der neuesten Zeit* (1939), p. 14, but Pound attributes it to Bernhard von Bülow in a letter of 1952: 'delighted to come in vBülow/ re some cardinal that he did not get elected pup/ because mit das Bankhaus Pacelli kompromettiert' – *'I Cease not to Yowl': Ezra Pound's Letters to Olivia Rossetti Agresti*, ed. Demetres Tryphonopoulos and Leo Surette (University of Illinois Press, 1998), p. 100. Sarti is a misspelling of (Giuseppe) *Sarto* (Pius X, pope 1910–14). The German quotation recurs on p. 58 of the typescript, with the addition: 'that was, who was it, when they put in the Venetian' (i.e., Pius X, born near Treviso in the Veneto). Pound shared widespread Fascist suspicion of Pius XII (expressed in 72/435: 'A Borgia would

be more likely than a Pacelli to houseclean'), and so he was quick to pounce on a phrase that suggested a possible (quite imaginary) connection with a bank. For the Chinese phrase see above, *L'arif est gai*. 'Solari', who returns with his memories of WW1 in canto 110, is likely Silvio Solari (1886–1945), who was 'Podestà' (mayor) of Rapallo in the years of Pound's residence there. The image of the water bug casting shadows on the bottom of a rock pool (*botro*), having first appeared in the 1942 fragment 'Now sun rises in Ram sign' (*Cantos*, p. 820), recurs in 87/594 and 91/636. Pound found it in Enrico Pea's novella *Moscardino*, which he translated. William Roscoe's *Life of Lorenzo de' Medici* (1796), I, p. 277, quotes Muratori on Lorenzo's style as 'gold from the mine, mixed indeed with ruder materials, yet it is always gold' – though this is not necessarily the passage that caught Pound's attention.

novis, nova remedia (p. 161)
A page of typewritten notes, dated '2 Jan' (1958), with additions from a reworking of the same materials on a page beginning 'this part is for adults'. The references to the Monarch butterfly were partly used in cantos 106 ('the king-wings in migration') and 109, and in the fragment 'La faillite de François Bernouard' ('the kings meet in their island' – *Cantos*, p. 821). The tribute to Laval and Pétain is a repeat from 76/480 (where only their initials appear); now Pound would even have them interred at Les Invalides, France's national pantheon. The anecdote regarding Draza Mihajlovitch is recorded in similarly obscure terms in 104/758. As he often does in the later cantos, Pound evokes the Na-khi or Naxi people of southwest China, a remote and then still pristine rural folk known to him through Peter Goullart's *Forgotten Kingdom* (John Murray, 1957) and Joseph Rock's scholarship. 'forméd trace' is from Pound's Cavalcanti ('Willing man look into that forméd trace in his mind' – 36/198, cf. 76/477).

Till Di Marzio cita (p. 163)
This passage (c. 1958–59) closes a typescript draft of canto 112, following the extract printed at 112/804–05 (under the heading 'From CXII'). It is mostly made of notes from the *Ricordi* of the Florentine historian Francesco Guicciardini, with some interpolations regarding US history, the Na-khi and their capital Lijiang. Cornelio Di Marzo was chief editor of the weekly *Meridiano di Roma*

at the time of Pound's collaboration. The themes listed as 'quoted' (*cita*) by Di Marzio in the second line are treated in cantos 96, 97, 98–99, 107–109 and 106, respectively. For the quotation from W. H. Hudson and 'ga dara agdu' see 94/655 and 97/698–99. The US economist Alexander Del Mar is one of the principal sources of the later cantos, especially 97. The Chinese characters and the drawing of the hawk (seal of Sargon the Great according to Pound's source, L. A. Waddell, *Egyptian Civilization: Its Sumerian Origin*, 1930, cf. 94/655) are not in the typescript, but Pound left blanks for their insertion. 'ta seu' (*Ta Hsio* or *Dà xué*, great learning) is the first of the Four Books, which Pound translated twice in English and once in Italian (see above, *To attract the spirits by the beauty of jade*). Durandus of St Pourçain, a contemporary of Dante, was a Dominican theologian. Among Pound's correspondents in 1955–59 was one John M. Cerruti. For 'akasa' see above, *Accade ogni mezzo secolo una meraviglia*.

Out of Earth into tree (p. 165)
Lines from Notebook 2 (late 1958), as reproduced in *Drafts & Fragments. Facsimile Notebooks 1958–1959* (Glenn Horowitz, 2010); transcript provided for this edition by Walter Baumann. Significantly, these lines – mostly related to the Na-khi – make explicit the phrase that claimed Pound's attention in the 'muan-bpo' ceremony (98/711, 112/804): 'We have not used the wrong names for objects'. For Peregrinus's pyre see 100/740. Julia Domna was the Roman empress at whose request Philostratus wrote *The Life of Apollonius of Tyana* (94/659). In Egypt Apollonius offered a sacrifice 'to Memnon of the Dawn'; he held that 'the soul is immortal'. (The Greek phrases are quoted also in 96/660.) 'Ou tis' is the Noman-Odysseus of the Pisan cantos.

And might be lost if I do not record them (p. 167)
Three pages of notes for 'canto 117', September–December 1959. The writing is more convoluted and hesitant than previously. Pound recalls unduly neglected writers and friends: the pseudonymous Essad Bey, author of a life of Stalin and of *Twelve Secrets in the Caucasus* (97/698); Remy de Gourmont; Albert Londres (104/759); 'Willy' (Henry Gauthier-Villars, see 76/473, 78/500, 80/523–24). This is a recurrent motif of this period ('Bunting and Upward neglected' – 110/801), though Pound admits that 'Willy' is no major figure. He

returns to the Na-khi, and wonders how the name is pronounced and transliterated. (It is in fact pronounced 'na-shee'.) Obsessed by the need to finish *The Cantos*, he notes that this, 'if necessary', could be a suitable finale. He cites a phrase he was fond of ('Every man has the right to have his ideas examined one at a time' – *Selected Prose 1909– 1965*, p. 355, from *Impact*, 1960), and notes that it is a 'nuisance to outlive one's intelligence' (implying that this is his case). He describes his plight as that of 'a sick mouse' and laments (as he had done in Pisa) his lack of compassion – a theme repeated at the end of canto 116. 'In meine Heimat kam ich wieder' is from a German folksong, famously misquoted in 115/814. The draft ends with a radiant image of Pound's return to Italy and with a quotation-invocation of a benevolent and 'serene' woman: 'O miracle of God who receives love, neither calumny nor envy touches you'.

the madness & cancer are nothing (p. 170)
These lines, from Notebook 6 (late 1959), follow upon the vision of Genoa at the close of the previous fragment. The source is the *Drafts & Fragments Facsimile*, transcribed by Walter Baumann. Some readings are doubtful. Pound writes despondently but seeks to reaffirm that 'beauty exists', as in the coeval canto 116 ('but the beauty is not the madness'). The blind Carlo Delcroix was president of the Italian Association of War Invalids; in 92/641 he is quoted as saying that he carries the blindness 'for I forget how many ten thousand Italians'. Zhu Ying's comment that Chinese and Japanese should be 'like brothers' appears also in the *ERIGENA* draft (above). It's not clear whether 'outside porta del Popolo' (a major landmark in Rome) qualifies the previous or the following line (in the latter case it might allude to the indifferent new buildings just north of the old Roman centre). 'How confess error' recurs at the end of canto 116 ('To confess wrong without losing rightness'). Pound goes on to declare his affection for a woman by quoting a line from *Lustra*: 'And Tibullus could say of his death, in his Latin: / "Delia, I would look on you, dying"' ('Impressions of François-Marie Arouet (de Voltaire)'. '*Atasal*' or '*ittisal*' (the latter being the correct spelling), mystical union in Arabic, is from Pound's Cavalcanti essay and from a central passage at 76/478: 'nor is this yet *atasal*'. In *After Strange Gods*, T. S. Eliot ('his Eminence') criticised Pound's Hell cantos 15–16 as 'disturbing to no one's complacency [...] a Hell for the *other people*'. Thiers's comment on the income tax as

'the portal to inquisition' is from 100/740. 'aged gem Fasa' and the city in the mind recall the African 'Lute of Gassir' tale ('Agada, Ganna, Silla! Hooh! Fasa!') of 74/430. The young woman who appears in 'flat shoes' and whose loss Pound laments is most likely Marcella Spann, who accompanied him to Italy in 1958 and returned to the US in September 1959. It is probably an occasion in her company that is referred to in the luminous vision of Genoa (mentioned above), since she spent the summer of 1959 with Ezra and Dorothy in Rapallo. Pound concludes with a rendering of thanks, a frequent gesture in the late drafts and cantos ('for the blue flash and the moments / benedetta' – 117/821). He owes such moments of peace and insight to the women who have given him affection and support.

VIII. LINES FOR OLGA 1962–1972

The order of the fragments in this section is conjectural. They are preserved among the papers of Olga Rudge, who from April 1962 was Pound's constant companion. The first fragment bears in the margin the title given to the section. Olga made copies of these texts in her notebooks. Her comments, some of them taped, are quoted below, marked 'OR'. The texts and comments in Olga's tapes and notebooks have been transcribed by Richard Sieburth.

& the grasshopper was not yet dead on his stalk (p. 175)
Manuscript. 'Written at Sant'Ambrogio' (OR). In canto 115 Pound describes himself as 'A blown husk that is finished'. Here he voices his sense of unexpected survival, entirely due to the generosity and strength of his companion. Edgardo Rossaro, a minor Rapallo artist, signed in February 1944, with Pound and others, a 'Manifesto of the Writers of the Tigullio', in support of the R.S.I. (Mussolini's 'Italian Social Republic' of Salò). The refrain 'sero, sero' ('late, late') is in canto 25 and in a 1942 fragment (*Cantos*, p. 819), but here rather suggests a belated admission of love. The ultimate source is Augustine, *Conf.* 10.27.38

The gondolas dying in their sewers (p. 176)
Rudge Notebooks, III, 136. 'A pencilled page written 26 November 1964. In America, Thanksgiving Day' (OR).

and as to why this timing? (p. 177)
Rudge Notebooks, III, 151–52. 'A note in pencil with no date [. . .].
Walking down the salita to Rapallo towards sunset, also the cherry
tree' (OR). For the most notable occurrence of the Sant'Ambrogio
'salita' (steep hill-path) see 80/520.

flood & flame (p. 178)
Manuscript. Pound speaks of the resilience of Olga, a small woman
of decision and elegance, who after her evenings and concerts in
Rapallo took the long solitary trek uphill to her quarters in 'Casa 60',
Sant'Ambrogio. In February 1927 Olga gave a private violin recital
for Mussolini, accompanied on the piano by Daniele Amfitheatrof –
see Anne Carson, *Olga Rudge and Ezra Pound* (Yale University Press,
2001), p. 71. Here Pound alludes to her assessment (possibly critical)
of the Duce (also an amateur violin player).

Olga's name being courage (p. 179)
Typescript, signed in longhand, dated 1965. Another rendering of
thanks. The opening statement recurs in a fragment sent by Pound to
his publisher James Laughlin on August 24, 1966, with the request
that it be placed at the close of *The Cantos*; Laughlin obliged in the
1995 paperback edition. Here Pound recalls some moments of his
forty-year-old partnership with Olga: an excursion to the Paris suburb
of Ville-d'Avray (97/700, and perhaps 80/529: 'where they set tables
down by small rivers'), her silhouette against the window ('contre-
jour') as she played the violin 'with the sea beyond making horizon'
(74/464), a snapshot of her on the beach of Santa Margherita (town
near Rapallo), and strolls on the Paris quays. According to Olga,
Pound had in mind their first meeting in autumn 1922: 'The walk
along the Seine ['Senna' in Italian] from rue Jacob 20 to 2 rue Cham-
fort [Olga's address] at 5 a.m. (?) after N. C. Barney's costume ball.
O.R. in Chinese coat belonging to Judith Gautier lent by Suzanne
Meyer & Chinese shoes lent by Arthur Frank's wife. E – black velvet
jacket & red Spanish cummerbund. Stopped for breakfast at café'
(OR). The feast of San Pantaleo, the small church near Olga's house
(to which she returned with Ezra in summer 1964), is held on the last
Sunday of July.

And there was nothing but water melon (p. 180)

Manuscript, one page. Olga made a longhand copy of this fragment, correcting the opening line. Pound had written: 'And there was no water mellon'. It is likely that he assented to her correction, since this must have been a story she told him of her own childhood ('Rudge family picnic on Mount Chocorua in 1903' – OR; Mt Chocorua is also mentioned in 74/460). The point is that Olga has always put up with adversity, and has willingly confronted difficult circumstances. The line about leaving a picnic for a funeral (OR: 'School picnic – Convent – Sherborne – Dorset') may be also a metaphor for her taking responsibility for Pound in his last years. *The Mousmé* ('The Little Japanese Mamma') was a 1911 musical by Lionel Monckton; Pound is alluding again to Olga's Chinese costume at their first meeting chez Natalie Barney. 'The climbing was on Costa Line ship – I had passage from Newport News – only it did not sail (coaling) after several days spent chez cousin Paul Maline – flew back to Italy – 1952' (OR). 'Red heart in a flask of perfume, i.e. a tiny red heart in a tiny flask of perfume I took to E.P. at Saint Eliz. in 1952, had bought it in Rapallo at the gift shop (il Porto?) by "penny-plain" and "tuppence coloured" sisters' (OR). Olga visited Pound at St Elizabeths on her birthday, April 13, 1952, and again in June 1955. The Wordsworthian touch of Olga's pity 'on every living thing' is a significant addition to the praise of her strength and courage. The reference to her having kept Pound alive 'for ten years' suggests that this homage may have been written after 1970, since Pound put himself in Olga's capable hands in April 1962, when his physical and mental health was indeed precarious, and both of them believed he was dying.

Index of First Lines